VOYAGE OF DREAMS

When Lolita decided it was time to write a brief family history to pass on as a legacy to her daughters, she never thought it would become a voyage of discovery for her. The secrets and hidden skeletons fascinated her, so Lolita delved deeper into old letters, documents and diaries. The brief history has become a book that is of interest not just to family and friends, but to the general public as well. Lolita's family history, including her own childhood, strikes her as being more unusual than what most folk experience.

Lolita will be publishing a follow-up book, *Life and Loves of Lolita*, which will relate how she lived her life to the full while single. It will include love letters she exchanged with her soldier sweetheart, who served in Vietnam.

VOYAGE OF DREAMS

Lolita Purins

ARTHUR H. STOCKWELL LTD
Torrs Park, Ilfracombe, Devon, EX34 8BA
Established 1898
www.ahstockwell.co.uk

© *Lolita Purins, 2021*
First published in Great Britain, 2021

The moral rights of the author have been asserted.

*All rights reserved.
No part of this publication may be reproduced
or transmitted in any form or by any means,
electronic or mechanical, including photocopy,
recording, or any information storage and
retrieval system, without permission
in writing from the copyright holder.*

*British Library Cataloguing-in-Publication Data.
A catalogue record for this book is available
from the British Library.*

Arthur H. Stockwell Ltd bears no responsibility
for the accuracy of information recorded in this book.

ISBN 978-0-7223-5089-8
*Printed in Great Britain by
Arthur H. Stockwell Ltd
Torrs Park   Ilfracombe
Devon EX34 8BA*

Settling down to look through a dusty, yellowing cardboard shoebox full of old letters stained brown from age, old curly sepia photos and various old documents, identity cards and postcards belonging to my mother and father, I started to unravel my essence. I began a journey of discovery. . . .

My great-uncle Rudolf O. Mikelsons was born in 1905 and became quite a celebrity in our family. When Rudolf was four years old he wanted to play a proper violin instead of the toy one he was given as a gift. In a temper, he stamped on it. He was born of Latvian parents. His mother, Kristine, took him to a violin maker, a relative who was well known for making instruments for many great musicians. His father, Roberts, died in the First World War. Rudolf showed a great gift for music, so a tiny violin was made specially for him. By the age of five he was giving concerts in palaces around the world. He was a child prodigy. He was awarded a scholarship to study music at St Petersburg Conservatory, which was founded in 1862 by Anton Rubinstein. The composer Nikolai Rimsky-Korsakov taught there for almost forty years. Rudolf was a student of the most prominent teacher in the world, Leopold Auer, who lived from 1845 to 1930. He was a Hungarian violinist, an academic, conductor and composer, but was best known as an outstanding violin teacher. He had many famous performers among his pupils and was professor of violin from 1868.

When Rudolf was a little older, the Tsar of Russia, Nicholas II, summoned the 'miracle' boy to the Winter Palace in St Petersburg and became like a second father to him. Rudolf became a playmate for the Tsar's youngest child, his only son, Alexei, born suffering from haemophilia on 12 August 1904.

Postcard of Rudolf produced in 1926.

The goldsmith to the imperial crown, Peter Carl Fabergé, designed fifty bejewelled Easter eggs for Alexander III and his son Nicholas II over three decades. Tsar Alexander presented his wife, Empress Maria Fedorovna, with seven eggs. She survived the revolution and came to England before returning to her native Denmark.

When Rudolf played at the palace and entertained young

Alexei, Nicholas was so grateful to him that he was gifted with some beautiful Fabergé. The location of the treasure remains a fascinating mystery.

As a young man, Rudolf married an Anna Anderson, but there are no details of this union. However, it is worth contemplating that the youngest daughter of Tsar Nicholas II was Anastasia Romanov, born on 18 June 1901. Her supposed assassination took place on 17 July 1918, during the Bolshevik revolution. It is claimed she survived as Anna Anderson, and was successfully smuggled out of Russia. Perhaps Rudolf played a part in this escape plot? Subsequent DNA test results are known to have been rigged.

Next, Rudolf studied in Paris with Lucien Capet (1873–1928), who was a French violinist, pedagogue and composer. He taught violin at the Societé Sainte-Cécile de Bordeaux. Rudolf then made a career for himself in Latvia as a concert violinist and conductor until he left the country.

The Soviet Union invaded Latvia in June 1940. When the Russians took over the three defenceless Baltic states, people were scared stiff and many went into hiding. People had to talk in whispers because the Russians started hauling them off to Siberia. Rudolf's family endured occupation for a while, but finally he and his second wife, Mirdza, a ballerina, decided they should leave. Nazi Germany invaded and occupied Latvia from 1941 to 1944. The Soviet Union then reoccupied the country. When the German forces were withdrawing in ships, they took with them women and children. Rudolf's mother, Kristine, remained in Riga, refusing to leave, but Rudolf put his son, Juris, on board a ship together with Mirdza, her mother and sister, and promised he would find them. That ship docked in Gdansk, Poland. The family then wandered into Germany with all their worldly goods on their backs and in dusty suitcases. They were bombed out of one city then another, travelling on foot, by cattle truck, and by any other available means. They remained in Germany from 1944 to 1949.

When the war ended, Rudolf arrived in Germany and went from one displaced-persons camp to another. He searched until he finally found his family in the British sector of Hanover.

Australia was busy recruiting labour, and they were promised free passage if they worked there for two years. They decided to accept. They docked in Adelaide, where they remained for eleven years.

Mirdza's sister, Nora Alksnis, had trained as a lawyer while in Germany, but never actually practised law in Adelaide. Instead she owned and operated a milk bar and never married. Mirdza and Nora's father was Valdemars Alksnis, a Supreme Court judge in Latvia. He also became a refugee in Australia.

Rudolf was fluent in Latvian, Russian, Polish, Ukrainian, German and English, so he worked as an interpreter in the personnel office of the Kelvinator Corporation. He couldn't continue his career in music as he wasn't an Australian citizen and therefore couldn't join the musicians' union. Basically, Australia was looking to employ 'mule skinners and opal miners'! However, Rudolf was able to perform in the Albert Hall, Canberra, when he had newly arrived in the country. This concert took place on 25 January 1950 and was billed as 'New Australians Make Music'. It was performed in front of an audience of 1,100 people.

Meanwhile, 9,000 miles away, a young violinist in the Indianapolis Symphony Orchestra was asked, by the conductor Izler Solomon, who had taught him to play so well? Solomon (1910–1987) led the Indianapolis Symphony Orchestra from 1956 to 1975. Unfortunately, a stroke in 1976 rendered him inactive. The young violinist told him that he had studied in Riga under a talented teacher and soloist named Rudolf Mikelsons.

A surprise letter arrived in Australia from Solomon, inviting Rudolf to join him in Indianapolis. This was an invitation he felt he could not refuse – he decided he had to accept. To make sure he hadn't lost his touch, he began to play his violin for sixteen hours per day, and this continued for many months.

After Rudolf arrived in the United States, he wrote to his family saying how much more 'civilised' that country was – they should all move there.

Rudolf's only son, Juris, who was born on 8 April 1937, studied music and journalism at college in Adelaide. He played the piano and the Spanish guitar. In January 1958 he wrote a letter to his cousin Rolands from Parkside in South Australia before he left the country. Juris described what had been happening to him while living there. As he had missed the last year of secondary school, he hadn't sat any exams. With no qualifications, he decided to become a taxi driver. After six months, he managed to purchase his own taxi only because it had a lot wrong with it. Then after eighteen months he had paid off the £1,400 it had cost him, including the radio, licence and shares in the company. His health hadn't been good, so a lot of his money had gone on medical bills. Then, after all that, he became a travelling salesman, promoting the latest American food mixer, which cost £38 cash. The job was OK, but after months of living in hotels 2,000 miles from home he was unhappy and longed to be back with his parents. He thought he ought to find a job in Adelaide, but his problem was that he didn't like to stay in one place for long. It's a big world and he felt restless. It was good that he could boast about Rolands owning a ship and being the captain: as Rolands could travel the world, perhaps he would consider having passengers and make his way to Australia, which was a popular destination for the English. Rolands was told to give his little friend Lolita an especially big kiss and to tell her not to call him *Uncle* Juri as he didn't have a grey beard yet. He said he couldn't wait to see them all again after so many years. He sympathised with Rolands that his marriage hadn't worked out at all. If she was really 'like that', Juris said, he would be better off without her and he should be grateful to be free from her. He added that he would love to hear more about the ship, including technical details, and even see some photos as that sort of thing was of great interest to him. He told Rolands Australia lacked 'culture' and the people lived like 'natives' – all they were interested in was the cinema, beer, horse racing and cricket!

Mirdza joined her husband in America in 1959. However, Juris wanted to see as much of the world as he could, and also visit his friends and relatives in England. He decided to join a merchant-marine ship. Finally he sailed to Jamaica, from where he flew to Toronto. He washed dishes for six months until his American visa came through. In August 1960 Juris joined his parents in Indianapolis.

Juris, 8 February 1960.

Having a strong lust for travel, Juris made the decision to become a pilot. In 1961 he was awarded instructor certificates for private and commercial flights, and just three years later he joined the Voyager airline as chief pilot and captain. He set foot in over eighty countries during his career.

For Rudolf's brother Janis, life and experiences were totally different. My grandfather Janis Juliuss Roberts Mikelsons was born on 23 February 1900 in Berzmuisa, Latvia. He spent his childhood in Flat 55, Lačpleša Road 59, Riga. His wife, Anna Irma Briedis, born in Penkule on 11 August 1906, was brought up in Flat 1, Valdemara Road 77, Riga.

When Janis married Anna they lived in a farmhouse in Lielvārde. The white building with a red roof was on elevated ground and could be seen from a distance. From their windows you could see the River Daugava. Their children, Rolands and Aiva, were brought up there. Rolands Rudolf Karlis Mikelsons was born in Riga on 18 November 1926 and was baptised and confirmed in the Dome Cathedral.

My mother, Aiva Ruta Mikelsons, was born in Riga City Hospital on 23 July 1928.

On the farm there were one large lake and two smaller ones. Every farm produced something different, and as they were self-sufficient there was no need to buy provisions from shops. Even during political changes people didn't go hungry. They made their own cloth with looms. Jewish tailors would come to the farms and help create clothes for them. Their produce was also sold in markets and the family's farm specialised in growing maize, which gave them a good income. Janis was a qualified diesel engineer, and he was involved in doing contract work for hydroelectric power stations, and also in the construction of riverboats and tugs.

Anna had wealthy parents who owned a lot of the family's valuables. Her mother, Doroteja, owned a kiosk and also imported agricultural equipment. They were also property owners in Zemgale, Latvia, and in Germany. Anna's grandfather was a partner in the Dresden china factory. The Kaiser awarded him a medal for the successful production of this beautiful china, and there is proof of this in a photo album that was buried with a jewellery box.

Janis's mother, Kristine, was very fond of Rolands but always called him by one of his middle names, Rudolf, shortened to Rudy. This was the reason Rudolf Mikelsons was shown as the owner of some of the land, and it wasn't in Rolands' name. She bought a piece of land adjoining the property in 1939. The family considered it an ideal investment for them as not only would it enlarge the overall amount of land already owned, but Rolands could build himself a house on it when older. He was too young to legally own land and they could only have him registered as the owner by using his middle name of Rudolf. The family owned land as far as the eye could see. It amounted to 13,826 hectares, and deeds show that it was part of property number 140F, all legally owned by Janis.

Rolands shared his birthday with Latvia's anniversary of independence, achieved on 18 November 1918, but lost in the Russian occupation of 1940. He was always busy. When not at school, he would help his mother on the farm and usually had little time to play with other children.

When he was a very young boy, the love of Rolands' life was a pet hen he had reared from a tiny chick. The little hen would follow him to school, and, if tired, she would rest on his head or shoulders. One day he was waiting for his hen to come out of the coop but there was no sign of her. He was very upset. Then, after lunch, one of the farmworkers told him that he had just eaten the little hen, and Rolands, devastated, ran off into the forest. His mother had to look for him and found him sobbing. The farmer thought it was amusing to play a prank, not realising how much the little boy loved his pet. Anna brought the little hen in her arms to Rolands, to show him all was well.

At school, to celebrate Independence Day, the pupils would march around the huge school playground then line up around the flagpole while the Latvian lag was hoisted. The national anthem was sung and the ceremony was conducted by the headmaster and priest. Everyone would sing and take part in the historical plays that they staged. Rolands remembered those times clearly and, when small, believed that the flag was raised in celebration of his birthday.

Anna and Janis inherited this farm, which extended into forestry, from her wealthy family.

Rolands managed to have some hobbies and interests and showed signs of being creative as he enjoyed making model aeroplanes. At the age of ten he liked to design shoes and also helped his father with boat designs. He also spent a lot of time with a leather worker as he was fascinated by the manufacture of suitcases and handbags. On the whole he didn't have time to waste and didn't have much to do with his sister either. Rolands' love of graphic design started at school.

Janis worked in Kegmus, at the largest hydroelectric plant of its type in Europe. He also owned a number of small workshops in the Salagriva area near the Estonian border and employed a number of men in boat construction and cargo transport work. As an employer, he would be regarded as an exploiter by the Russians; so when they invaded, the family were under immediate threat.

In 1940 the family had to abandon their farm and literally move into the forest, living underground, like many other farmers. They dug holes so deep that the Russians, even with their dogs, were unable to find them. As a boy, Rolands found it exciting living underneath the fir trees. Every farmer had enough stores of pickles and preserves in their hideouts to be able to survive. Fish was pickled and meat was salted and they were able to exist quite comfortably. Unfortunately, they had to let their animals roam free, and the deserted farms were looted. This decision to stay hidden saved the family from deportation and even death, which was the fate of so many others.

'Our tunnel was deep and well organised. My father made up a caustic soda solution to keep our dogs away.'

The winters were severe and the farm could be cut off due to heavy snowfalls. Because he was young, Rolands found it all 'absolutely fascinating' and didn't think about it the way adults would. They spent three months underground and managed to save some of their valuables by sealing them in greased metal casks, which they buried deep in the ground. Everything was well packed and protected to ensure their survival for hundreds of years if necessary. There was silverware, crystal, fancy goods, amber and coins – even a pure-silver pistol was among the buried treasure, which could still be there, undiscovered. . . .

The Russians invaded as one large army, but then divided up into smaller groups so that they could spread themselves around Latvia and keep an eye on the people. The soldiers were not fed enough and you could do nothing to stop them looking for food and robbing properties. They were shabby, with worn-out shoes and very plain uniforms with no embellishments. They didn't hesitate to rape the women, shoot people, and ship out successful men, such as engineers and doctors, to Siberia or elsewhere in Russia. Or they made use of their knowledge before shooting them. My family did not manage to avoid Russian brutality. When the Russians were losing their front line to the Germans, they were in need of boats to ferry their soldiers across the Latvian rivers. My grandfather was well known in the nautical industry and was informed upon by a friend of his, whose family were threatened with death if they did not disclose information. The Russians found Janis, who had ventured out to check the farm, and he was taken to the River Daugava to assist with the crossings. However, he found he was unable to operate many of the boats because the engines had been tampered with. Not willing to help the enemy, he began to throw any spare engine parts into the water. So the soldiers started knocking him about. They didn't shoot him as he could still be of use and they might need his skills. Their treatment of Janis was horrific. He was beaten up so badly that he lost an eye, and then they scarred his body with red-hot iron bars.

'He suffered tremendously.'

He was detained for two days and was in no state to return to the forest, so he was loaded into a cattle wagon with other unfortunate men. Enemy planes flew overhead and opened fire. This was a chance to escape; and while the soldiers took cover, Janis and another man managed to scramble to nearby bushes. This was a very lucky move for them as they soon realised that those crammed in the wagons were destined to be shot.

The family, still in hiding, were totally unaware of what had been happening to Janis. He managed to drag his battered, burnt body back to their hideout. Anna took charge of nursing him and did her best to apply first aid in spite of limited resources. It was a good job they had a large bottle of iodine to help keep the wounds from becoming infected. They felt sick when they first saw him and could only wait, hope and pray that Janis would survive.

In just one year of being occupied, Latvia was a changed country. There were more soldiers than ordinary folk. Looting was rife. The Russians took the best homes and the best furniture. The nicer your home was, the more dangerous it was for you. The soldiers had such a primitive attitude and behaviour, it made them even more frightening.

'Dead bodies would be seen hanging from trees, always with a note pinned to the corpse stating that this punishment was to set an example.'

It was a nightmare time. Anna used to cut people down from the trees so that they could be buried and laid to rest. The NKVD, the communist Russian secret police, would shoot innocent people in the street just for their amusement. You had to do what they told you as the second choice was to disappear to a concentration camp.

The family survived the occupation. When the Germans invaded, everyone emerged from their underground homes and resumed a somewhat normal life. The German army were more disciplined; and if a soldier dared to rape, he was shot. However, when the Gestapo entered the country the soldiers became more cruel and strict. If you were a Gypsy or Jewish, you would have been disposed of. Although they removed all the livestock, the landowners still had plenty of supplies of preserved food.

In 1943 Rolands was recruited and forced to leave Latvia. He repaired boats at Hamburg Docks while living in barracks. He was sent to nautical college at Würzburg as his skills were regarded as 'advantageous' to the German army. He also helped to repair damaged trains while living near the railway station. Anyone involved in communications was useful, like Janis was to the Russians. As one of the 'chosen few' Rolands was supposed to be trained to fight in the Nazi army, but he managed to escape from the college in desperation to search for his parents.

When he was in the Brandenburg area, he found work in a German truck factory. After three weeks there, he saw a chance to leave. He made plans with a young Italian who also worked there. The area was being constantly bombed and their plot was to make sure the factory was destroyed: they turned all the wing mirrors of the trucks towards the sky. The reflection meant the bombers could locate the factory from the air, and it was successfully destroyed. Both men made it to the river and had to swim across to the west. Rolands made it to the other side, but nearly drowned. Some Estonian refugees took him to a hospital where he needed to have water drained out of him. After recovering, he travelled to Kitzingen with some Poles. They found a cellar to hide in that was away from the bombings by the British and Americans, who destroyed the city. They were in total darkness. The pipes had been broken and hot water rose around them. Then a huge explosion blew in the side of the cellar. They escaped and were very lucky to survive.

Rolands found two stranded children in the debris and wondered what would be the right thing to do with them. They were only three and five years old and were 'delightful'. Although weak, Rolands managed to carry them, one under each arm, and searched for a suitable shelter and also some food. After the bombings, grocery stock was scattered everywhere and he didn't hesitate to fill his pockets. He understood from the children that their father had been taken away by the Germans. They liked their new 'uncle' and were always watching him to make sure they didn't lose him. Eventually, a kind German lady and her Latvian friend befriended them and offered their hospitality and a bed for the night. It was the first proper bed Rolands had seen for a long while. Being unused to its softness, he was found sleeping on the floor when his breakfast was brought to him in the morning. The generous couple took the children into their care.

When the Germans were leaving Latvia because the Russians decided to invade again in 1944, my family decided it was time to leave their homeland for good. For safety, they travelled separately. The farmhouse was bombed by the Russians and completely destroyed. Rolands had no idea where his parents and sister had disappeared to.

A hundred and forty thousand Latvians fought on the German side during the Second World War. They were drafted into the Waffen SS and believed they were all fighting for Latvia to be independent again. In recent times, Latvian SS veterans insist they were not party to any atrocities. As young men they believed they were fighting for their country. But the real beneficiary of the men's service and bravery was Nazi Germany.

Some Latvian refugees managed to reach Sweden, where they were content to settle. My family had made it safely to the Central Latvian Displaced-Persons Camp in Würzburg, West Germany. They then transferred to a smaller displaced-persons camp in Greven V18, which was a Latvian group in a British sector of Germany. At long last, with the help of the International Red Cross, Rolands was reunited with them in 1945. From 1945 to 1946 he taught art in the camp and also organised exhibitions. His address at that time was 43 Colping Strasse. He was also employed as a policeman.

In 1946 they were offered passage to Great Britain, where Rolands settled and made his life secure. He was intent on keeping his sentimental, valuable belongings on him. He managed to leave Germany with items that belonged to his grandfather, such as a large twenty-four-carat-gold pocket watch with a heavy-duty twenty-four-carat-gold chain attached. He also had a twenty-four-carat-gold ring inset with a square jewel, solid-gold cufflinks and sterling-silver cufflinks engraved with monograms. He had saved his baby silver cup and spoon engraved with his name, as well as photos from his great-grandparents' day, and of his father in his shipping business. They were stored in Latvian handmade leather albums embossed with ethnic symbols.

Aiva, together with her mother, Anna, arrived in Wales, where they were employed as nursing assistants in Cefn Mably Hospital, in December 1946.

Cefn Mably Hospital, 7 December 1946.

Situated in the St Mellons area of Cardiff, it was originally a manor house leased by Lord Tredegar to the NHS for use as a tuberculosis sanatorium. (After it closed down in 1983, it became derelict, then was destroyed by fire.)

Aiva carried an identity card which showed the route she took around Great Britain, and the addresses where she lived. I can't help but wonder if this mother-and-daughter team were made aware of the health risks they took when accepting employment in this country.

Anna and Aiva.

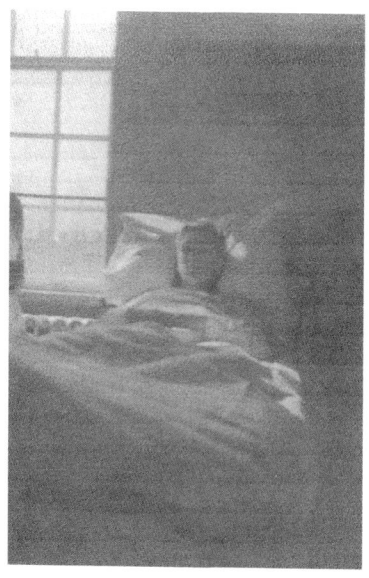

Aiva.

Their next location, a year later, in September 1947, was the general hospital in Tamworth, which is now the Old Cottage Hospital in Hospital Street. In the 1940s, epidemics such as scarlet fever raged through the town. There were no vaccines to prevent this disease. In April 1948, while living in Tamworth, Aiva caught scarlet fever and was hospitalised for about ten weeks. Meanwhile, Rolands found himself living in the WAEC Hostel, Grendon Road, Tamworth, and worked as a farmer from 1947 to 1949. When Aiva was allowed home from hospital, she had to make weekly visits to the doctor, and was kept on medication for a long time. She should have been hospitalised again, but chose instead to stay at home and remain in bed. Being unable to work, she decided to move to Wallasey, a town in Merseyside. As it was close to the Liverpool dock area, it is possible that both Janis and Rolands were employed in the shipyard and they were all living close to each other. Rumours of asbestosis in the men may be true as Liverpool dock workers were heavily exposed to the asbestos dust.

During the Second World War every Latvian was prepared to fight in order to prevent the Russians from returning to Latvian territory. The whole Latvian population ardently desired the restoration of the Latvian National Army, and the formation of the Latvian Legion in 1943 seemed to serve as the first step. Many believed that German occupation meant that Latvia would then regain its independence, and that belief was exploited by the Germans in the first weeks of occupation. Those dreams were short-lived though. Latvians joined forces with the Germans against the Russians because they regarded the ruling communist regime in Moscow as the biggest threat to their hopes of re-establishing an independent, prosperous Latvia. They wanted to fight against the imperial power of the USSR. The Nazis moved quickly to secure firm control over all aspects of Latvian political life. They chose to exploit the economic and human resources there.

Baltic nationals in the Latvian Legion have not been regarded as war criminals or traitors. The only charge against them was that they fought against the Soviet armed forces.

In addition, the German Nazi army particularly liked Latvians as they were regarded as Aryan, and in general made suitable soldiers ethnically. The army would visit the high schools in Riga to cherry-pick all the brightest students. The idea was to create a perfect race. Young men like Rolands were selected to be among the 'chosen few', and they were given special training to fight alongside the Nazis. A friend of the family, Alfons Kudins, was a legionnaire and admitted to his own family in South Wales that as he was from a well-off family he was hand-picked from his boarding school. He didn't have much choice. He witnessed a lot of terrible things when only nineteen years old; and although he hadn't performed any atrocities himself, his wife destroyed all photos of him in uniform.

My father, Zigfrids Heinrichs Purins, was born on 21 September 1924 in Gaujmalnieki, in the Sēja area of Riga. There is no information about his childhood. In 1939 he passed school exams in geography, art, chemistry, biology, archaeology, physics, Latvian, English and German. He was brought up with his twin sister, Hilda, in Murjāni near Sigulda. Their parents also farmed their own land.

The twins, Hilda and Zigfrids.

The Wehrmacht was the unified armed forces of Nazi Germany from 1935 to 1946, consisting of the army, navy and air force.

In the Second World War, the Wehrmacht was an outstanding force – one of the greatest in history. Officially it was forbidden to conscript the inhabitants of Latvia to serve in its military forces, but the rule was circumvented. At the age of twenty-one, Zigfrids was 'involuntarily conscripted' into the Wehrmacht. Most Latvian soldiers in Germany were at first kept in British POW camps there. In the autumn of 1945 most were transferred to POW Camp 2227 at Zedelgheim, in Belgium.

On 6 November 1945 Zigfrids found himself in Camp 2227. The Latvian men had naïvely expected the Western Allies to understand the reasons they fought on the side of the Germans; but instead of understanding, they received beatings. At times they were used for live target practice by the guards. They were released during 1946, when the Western Allies concurred that the Latvians were not Nazis despite their SS uniforms. The town is now working to save and preserve for posterity the remaining fragments of POW Camp 2227 so that the story of what happened there can be told for generations to come. It is a story which tells of the Latvian spirit and will to survive.

In June 1946 Zigfrids was discharged from the army. His D2 'control form' showed his occupation as 'car driver', and he was moved to the displaced-persons camp in Schwarzenbek, Germany. Then the following year he was living in Flensburg Displaced Persons Camp, where there was an active Latvian community. In displaced-persons camps, life was generally simple, with no worries. There was little to eat though the provisions were better in the American zone as they were able to distribute army surplus. In the British zone, Latvians were living in a mini version of Latvia. They had their own schools and church services. There was no need to leave the camp and everyone was basically happy. Also in the Flensburg Displaced Persons Camp was a very pretty teenager called Lolita. She was fun-loving, and she and Zigfrids became good friends, enjoying each other's company. She was also dating other young men. However, her family were offered passage to Canada, and Lolita went with them. There she was reunited with one of her boyfriends from the camp, and they became engaged after just a week.

The theatre group in Flensburg Displaced Persons Camp, December 1947. Zigfrids (third row, second from left) was one of the performers.

In 1948 Zigfrids had just qualified as a third engineer after his final exams at the Navigation and Sea Engineering School for displaced persons, and decided to head for England. By 1949 countries were offering work to people from the Baltic States. England favoured single men to work in the coal mines; Canada offered housekeeping duties to young and middle-aged women; the USA took a few families who would be involved in church organisations; and Australia was keen to select whole families to settle there, to help populate the country.

From 1948 to 1951 Zigfrids was employed as a mechanic for the Pelton Steamship Co. Ltd, based in Newcastle upon Tyne. In July 1949 he decided to enrolled in the National Union of Seamen so that he could also serve on the SS *Ramava*, which was owned by Pelton Ltd. In the merchant navy he was able to see many countries and took many photos which show he made the most of his travels.

Zigfrids, newly qualified in Flensburg, 13 January 1948.

SS Ramava, *the ship Zigfrids served on.*

In June 1951 Zigfrids was discharged from the merchant navy by the Mercantile Marine Office, and in the October he moved to Milford Haven to join his future wife, Aiva.

Zigfrids with his shipmates, entertaining with his much loved accordion.

Zigfrids (right).

Zigfrids (middle) enjoying free time on the Italian Riviera in April 1949.

In October 1949 Aiva had moved to 6 Fairfield Street in Liverpool, and she lived there with Rolands until May 1950. It was at a gathering of Latvian refugees that she met Zigfrids. She was still taking medication and later reminded him that he probably recalled she had 'sunburn', a symptom of scarlet fever. Unfortunately, she never fully recovered and went on to develop rheumatic fever, as treatment was not always effective. Regular X-rays were carried out as the illness can cause heart problems. Emotional instability can also be a permanent side effect, which may explain why Aiva always seemed such a sensitive soul.

Tied with blue ribbon, a bundle of love letters had been safely stored away from Zigfrids' eyes. They revealed a love story spanning from November 1948 until July 1949. Aiva, as a young woman of twenty years, was exchanging letters with a young man called Rudis, who lived in Birdingbury, near Rugby. In his early letters he complained that he couldn't concentrate on anything at all as his thoughts were entirely about her, even though he hardly knew her. They had met on a Saturday when he was playing the accordion in a Latvian dance band. Aiva had told him that the only days she didn't tell untruths were Saturdays, so he wished every day was a Saturday! Rudis was totally captivated by this petite dark-haired girl with a Gypsy wildness about her. He asked if he could collect her the following Saturday from the bus station in Coventry. He said he would be waiting impatiently for her reply. A week later he wrote again, saying that although he had only known Aiva for a few days, it felt like a few years. He wanted her to be with him. There had been a time when he believed no girl would ever turn his head, but then one night he met Aiva. He wished he could have danced with her all night, but he had to play his accordion as well.

'Please come tonight, and place your little hand on my feverish brow . . .'

By January Rudis had proclaimed his love for her, but perhaps he loved her too much. In February he was stressing about the words they had exchanged during their date, but he said he would be totally lost without her. Until then he had only lived for today and the thought of anything more permanent made him uneasy. However, by the end of the month Rudis said he never wanted to lose her. He always signed off his letters with many kisses to his '*mazais kukainis*' (i.e. his little insect). In the April he decided to open up his heart to her. Rudis explained that he had come to England to escape the memory of a lost love in Latvia. Then he found someone else – someone who doubted his sincerity, but who really did mean more to him now than ever before. He had declared his love, but she never said those words back to him. . . . That girl was his own little Aiva. She was not to shed any tears over him as he could never deceive her. In mid April he thanked her for being more open to him in her letter. He begged her not to leave him when she told him she was planning to go to Australia with her family. He felt that when they were together she lacked the confidence to open up to him. He thought she found it easier to express her true feelings in her letters to him. Rudis had lost his parents and lived alone, unlike Aiva. He felt that she would find life difficult if they were together, and he could never forgive himself if her life was hard because of him. However, he still tried to dissuade her from leaving by saying Australia would be difficult to get used to, and Latvians were not suited to the climate there.

In May, Aiva was unwell for a while, so he started to visit her at home. Then, in June, Rudis's letters became sorrowful. He had revealed to her all his deepest thoughts and complained that she wasn't being open with him again. His normally neat handwriting was in disarray. She was a good listener, yet told him very little. Perhaps he was expecting too much from her. He described Aiva as being dear, sincere, a good girl, but often childlike too. He believed she would like to express her feelings, but she didn't. By the end of June, Rudis decided to say he was now being 'honest' with her and tell her that, actually, she could never be happy with him. He said they were just too different as people to ever understand each other. He hoped they would always be friends. On 1 July Aiva received another love letter from Rudis. She was as dear to him now as she was in the beginning. However, he now realised that she was a far more serious person than he was. There always seemed to be a 'barrier' between them. She had always been dear, sincere and polite, but she had never been really open with him. He arranged to meet her as usual, in Dordon. In reality though, he wanted to have the strength to leave her so that she would no longer be unhappy with him. Rudis wrote a few more letters and felt sadness as she was no longer writing back to him. He continued to play in the band, but he said nothing felt the same any more.

Rudis's very last letter to Aiva, in time for her twenty-first birthday, was in response to Aiva accusing him of nailing up his heart. He agreed with her, adding that he could only blame himself, and his future looked empty. He would visit her again one Sunday; but if that caused her discomfort, he would feel rejected and would never write again.

At the end of 1950 Aiva moved with her family to Milford Haven. Only then did her health improve enough for her to cope with light household duties, and she came off her medication.

Janis, Aiva, Rolands and Anna – a family photo taken before they all left Liverpool in 1950.

In 1950 the R. S. Hayes Dockyard in Pembroke Dock, West Wales, was full of ex-naval craft of all types, ranging from small gunboats to corvettes and light cruisers. Among these lay the German E-boat *95*. She was a real beauty, sleek and extremely fast with three twenty-four-cylinder 3000-h.p. Mercedes-Benz marine engines. An E-boat is a German 'enemy boat', a motor torpedo boat with a top speed of forty-three knots (50 mph), the fastest thing afloat in the 1940s.

E-boat 95.

The length was 115 feet, and the breadth was seventeen feet six inches. It was sometimes referred to as the 'greyhound of the sea'.

Rolands chose to purchase the smaller craft, and thus began what became a saga of endurance. He was able to examine her by arrangement with the Admiralty agent in the docks. At low tide, the ships lay on the mud, and Rolands, wearing waders, had to trek across the mud. But when trapped by the incoming tide he had to swim ashore.

The Certificate of Purchase from the Director of Navy Contracts, of the Admiralty in Bath, showed the E-boat, weighing sixty tons, as having the official number of T19. She was built by Schichau, a German engineering works and shipyard based in East Prussia, in October 1938. She was originally launched on 20 July 1940. The boat was returned to Bremen in Germany for a refit in 1943 to '44. She was then reassigned to the torpedo school and returned to active duty. She did convoy escort duties, mine-laying missions and finally, on 5 May, ferried 45,000 refugees from Germany to Denmark, then 20,000 refugees on 9 May. The boat was transferred to the United States as war reparation (compensation for the victors of war), then sold to Denmark in 1947 for $5,000. After that, she was never used and finally was scrapped in 1950 to 1951.

Bitter disappointments, setbacks and frustrations followed the commencement of work on the vessel, which was named *Aiva* until her departure from Milford Haven. Janis was at sea during this time, working on the Estonian steamship *Torne*, which was over 2,000 tons and sailed from Dakar to Bristol. She carried special grass for making cigarette papers. He was paid off and was able to join his son in Milford Haven. After the stark and tragic horrors of the war they had escaped, the boat became their sole reason for living, and that preserved their sanity. Only 140 of these boats survived the war to become part of the spoils of war. Just eleven ended up in Great Britain, and one of those was in the hands of my family.

In January 1952, in Milford Haven, the boat was being converted in a ship-breaker's yard. She was to become a motor yacht/houseboat and was worked on in the sheltered creek of Castle Pill, which was accessed from Cellar Hill via the Pill Waterway. Her insurance value in February 1950 was £5,000, and the estimate rose to £8,000 after the complete refit. In March 1957 the boat was renamed MV *Tobago* and then she made the journey from Milford Haven to West Dock, Cardiff.

Sailing from Milford Haven.

Also in West Dock was a boat called *Margaret*. The owner, Danny Griffiths, can remember the *Tobago* being berthed halfway along the west side. Sadly he never saw or met any of those on board.

Rolands claimed to be very religious and said God had helped him through the trauma of the war years. None of the family felt settled in Great Britain, and, with that thought in mind, Rolands decided to investigate new destinations for them. They would be able to use their newly converted houseboat to reach a new country they could make their home in. With that aim, Rolands bought himself a ticket and is shown on a passenger list on a ship travelling to Montreal, Quebec, in 1954. As many Latvians had created new communities in Toronto, Ontario, he decided to head there.

In a short time he met and fell in love with a young lady, twenty-three years of age, called Rasma Silders. She had sailed from Southampton on the TSS *Columbia*, which was bound for Montreal on 12 June 1950. She travelled with her brother Raimonds. A 'Statement of Marriage' certificate shows that their wedding took place on 4 December 1954 in the city of Toronto. The bachelor and spinster were described as being Evangelical Lutheran, both born in Latvia. He was described as being a marine engineer, and she was a clerk. Rasma's parents were Fricis Silders and Ida Zakis, and their witnesses lived in 9 Bowden Street, Toronto. Rolands, now aged twenty-seven, lived at 47 Hilton Avenue in Toronto from September 1954 to April 1955.

Shortly after their wedding, Rolands left her to return to Wales. He was shown on the passenger list of a Cunard ship called RMS *Ascania*. He boarded the ship in Halifax and gave his address as 'M/V, Lower Coombes, Milford Haven, Pembrokeshire'. His marital status was M, indicating he was a married man. He had promised to return to Rasma, but he never did. The separation dragged on until it was obvious that he would never be returning to Canada. Rasma was never supposed to go to England and didn't want to. Looking back at their marriage, she was very bitter about what happened.

It was sheer coincidence that Rasma and Lolita, Zigfrids' ex-girlfriend, became the best of friends. Lolita described her as being 'sexy', always well dressed and fashionable, with immaculate hair and make-up, and said she never looked 'motherly'. Also, she wasn't tired or stressed by having children and was obviously no 'plain Jane', unlike some of her married friends. Yet Rolands told her he had to return to work, 'painting ships'. He stubbornly refused a divorce, so she was stuck in a loveless, lonely marriage. He robbed her of her best years as she was not free to meet someone else and have a child. By the time he agreed to divorce her, twenty years later, it was too late and she remained childless. Further details are not available as Rasma and Lolita are the closest of friends and fiercely loyal to each other. Rolands never spoke about his wife. However, in a diary he briefly mentioned his marriage, which only lasted three months. He claimed he didn't get the chance to learn 'what is good married life'. He hated abuse and nasty swear words. He added that perhaps his next marriage would offer everything he needed(?). He liked to give and receive a lot of love. Good food was a pleasure, but the only cooking he had ever done was in his Scouting days. He had decided his marriage was an unhappy experience and he vowed to live like a saint because of that, without any romantic or physical involvement. Rolands was, in his own words, 'deeply hurt and disappointed'. But he did keep his twenty-four-carat-gold wedding ring as a souvenir. As for Rasma, she went on to meet Romualds Lukasevics and they have been happily married for many years.

In January 1958 Rolands' cousin Juris wrote to him calling him an 'old sea wolf'. He sympathised over Rolands' failed marriage and tried to be reassuring, saying that amongst women there are devils as well as angels. He was not to lose hope as it was possible to find an angel.

Tobago *moored in West Dock, Tiger Bay, Cardiff.*
Rolands is shown as captain.

In July 1951 Aiva discovered she was expecting a baby out of wedlock, which must have been quite a shock in those times. Then in January 1952 Zigfrids was admitted to Sealyham Hospital, from where he wrote fifty-five letters to Aiva until June 1952. First of all they were addressed to Aiva using her maiden name of Miss A.

Mikelsons. They then changed to Mrs A. Purins when Aiva gave birth on 4 April 1952 in Priory Hospital, Haverfordwest. Zigfrids was now generally known as Ziggy.

Sealyham Hospital was sited in the town of Wolf's Castle, between Haverfordwest and Fishguard in Pembrokeshire. Originally it was Sealyham Mansion, a Georgian country house with its own 100-acre secluded woodland estate. It was converted into a tuberculosis hospital and sanatorium with thirty beds from 1923 until 1954. In 1955 it was converted for the use of geriatric patients, then in 1964 it was permanently closed as a medical facility.

Ziggy's first letter to Aiva was loving, written to his 'darling'. He was trying to find out what was wrong with him, and what the results were from all the examinations and tests, but he was more concerned about her morning sickness. Apparently, he was told he did not have tuberculosis, so he asked if he could go home. He was very relieved that he had nothing seriously wrong with him. The doctor had also said that his lungs were fine and all he needed was rest. However, when he told the doctor that he did not want to be there any longer than a month, the doctor just smiled and left.

Ziggy stated that he would not be happy anywhere in the world if Aiva was not with him. He felt he was the luckiest person to have found his life's soulmate in her. Also, he said he would feel so much better if he knew that she didn't spend her days in tears, but lived a life of contentment. It seems he didn't have the necessary nightwear and toiletries for his hospital stay. Although he could ask one of the ward assistants to buy him the cheapest soap, he didn't want people knowing how poor he was. Ziggy compared Aiva to an oyster buried in sand, but also creating a 'precious pearl'. He reminded her of how important were faith, hope and love.

At the end of January, Ziggy wrote to say that her visit seemed to last only a moment although she was there for a couple of hours. Aiva was like a bright comet in the darkness, and he had no idea what he would do without her. He had to squeeze back the tears at the thought of their future together. They had their own star to light up their path, to give them the strength to face whatever difficulties life threw at them. The doctor had been to see him and reprimanded him. When Dr Davies had visited them on the boat, he had diagnosed pleurisy, but, instead of resting as instructed, Ziggy had carried on working. He should have done only the lightest of tasks and should have sat down more. The doctor informed him that if he'd had the three weeks' complete bed rest, he would not have needed to be hospitalised. Ziggy was shaken up by that, and he couldn't gather his thoughts together.

When the lights were out, he could see the sky from his bed. Ziggy imagined one of the stars to be his loved one and turned into a honeybee to visit him at night. Every moment was filled with thoughts of her.

He asked Aiva to bring his books, which included the Spanish book, a dictionary, and a notebook. He also needed to revise his navigational skills. He told her he felt much better – he no longer wheezed – and he believed the medication was helping. He managed to do some English-language studies as well. They would be testing him again for tuberculosis. Also, his passport had to be extended. Ziggy also asked if the men (her brother and father) had been working on the boat improvements. A big worry was that Aiva carried all the burden on her shoulders alone. As he was her lifetime soulmate, he should be there to support her and to help her overcome life's challenges. He felt like a bird with broken wings, unable to help himself let alone anyone else, but perhaps these obstacles were meant to test them. His love for her was as big as the world, but he was unable to show her. If they were strong together then they could overcome any problems, he told her.

The night nurse had given Ziggy the result of the tuberculosis analysis, which showed he was clear. However, there were some shadows in his left lung. If he ate well and had plenty of sleep, then all would be good. He felt very lucky that Aiva could visit him once a week, even if only for two hours. She was not to bring him preserves and fresh fruit. Because of their dire finances, he would prefer to have the money to enable him to buy writing paper, envelopes, postage stamps and a newspaper, which all added up to around five shillings. He would also appreciate her thoughts on the letter he planned to write to Canada. There were people there who had promised to give him a helping hand. It would be useful if he could include two photos of the boat – one taken at the beginning of their work on her, and one from the summer.

Ziggy believed he would be in hospital for at least six weeks before being assessed to decide what would happen in the next stage of his treatment. He felt that he was looked down on as he had no money. But people didn't understand his circumstances. He had to pay for the boat, deal with the tradesmen, and generally make sure the boat was seaworthy. When Aiva's mother thought Ziggy was well off, she was polite to him. Perhaps if he'd been legally her husband, everyone might have been more tolerant. He made the decision that he and Aiva had to arrange a ceremony to prevent him being shunned. However, there would never be peace and harmony while they all lived together under the same roof.

Ziggy had also been exchanging letters with his old school friend Valdis Briedis, who was living in Buenos Aires and suggested that the country might suit Ziggy as his next home. However, Valdis decided to emigrate to Canada in August 1957, with his family.

Ziggy was concerned about Aiva and wondered if she was still suffering with morning sickness. No doubt the baby was kicking strongly. How were things at home? He longed for them to be living independently, especially when the baby arrived. He also mentioned his skills in navigation, and that the captain of the SS *Ramava* had told him that, with all his knowledge, Ziggy could sail any ocean.

At the end of February Ziggy and Aiva planned a mystery outing. He had asked the staff for permission to leave the hospital for a couple of hours and to arrange a taxi as he wasn't allowed to walk much. He asked Aiva if she could bring him a tie and his yellow shirt, even though it might be a little tight as had put on weight – also spare money, just in case.

On 3 March Ziggy wrote to say he had at last been given the go-ahead by his doctor to travel to Haverfordwest on Wednesday. He would meet her at their arranged time. Hopefully the matron would sort out transport for him. His fellow patients advised him to arrange an ambulance as that would be free of charge. Aiva was not to forget the documents. (At no point was the purpose of their rendezvous mentioned.)

Then on 6 March 1952 there was a letter from Ziggy to say how blessed they had been to have such lovely weather the day before. He wondered if Aiva had reached home safely. Had anyone congratulated her, or had her family resented the news that the wedding had taken place? But not to worry if the latter had happened. A plush ceremony would not have made any difference to their disapproval. If their feelings towards him hadn't changed, then he hoped that one day they would be ashamed of themselves. There is a saying that you reap what you sow. Their future together would now be dependent on their ability to overcome all difficulties. When they had grown old and grey, they would see that however hard their marital start was, it had been based on a 'solid gold' foundation and on certainty. At the moment his health and finances were poor, but that would be overcome. Ziggy also thought it was a good thing they were having a baby now, as who knew how things would be in Argentina? They had both survived the atrocities of war and could now be joyful that they would be creating their own future. He felt so very happy that all had gone well the day before. He wondered if Aiva had mentioned to her family that he'd had a letter from Argentina. He didn't want to be the one responsible for trying to arrange their journey as that would only give them more reason to criticise him. Aiva was also to whisper to the little one that it mustn't kick so much!

The outing had drained him of all his strength and Ziggy was very relieved to get back into his hospital bed. His leg muscles ached so much that they were tender to the touch and the matron had forbidden him to get out of bed. No longer could they hide their marriage as there would be an announcement in the newspaper. He had told everyone that he had been married a while, but the paperwork wasn't in English. The patients liked to gossip and would soon notice that he didn't have any visitors. He didn't expect Aiva to travel such a long way with the baby – it was nearly twenty miles. She was not to worry about it as he would cope with their queries and suspicions.

On 13 March Ziggy commented that it was only a couple of

weeks until the baby came into the world. He was concerned as to how his 'darling' was doing. Had she been to the doctor? Were her legs still swollen? And did she still suffer from morning sickness? He didn't think it would be wise of her to visit him on Sunday. From her letters he sensed that there had been more tension at home, even though Aiva hadn't said so as such. She had difficulty hiding things from him so she had to be more open with him. He could tell that her life was not easy on board the boat and so wished he could be of more help.

On the 16th Ziggy wrote to say he was really worried that he hadn't heard from his darling wife. Had something happened to her? He begged her to please write even if only a couple of words. But there was no more correspondence until 8 April.

On 4 April the baby was born.

Ziggy had managed to arrange a visit to Aiva and their new baby, who were in Priory Hospital in Haverfordwest.

In his next letter, Ziggy said he wondered how they were both faring. Was she breastfeeding or did she have to build up her strength? He had thought that Aiva looked well. Was the baby putting on weight and how did she look? He would really like to see his daughter again soon and could only hope that he would be allowed out of hospital the following week. Ziggy didn't like to keep asking the doctors for permission, but he wasn't supposed to leave the hospital until he was healthy. He advised Aiva that if she was offered a period of convalescence, she should not scorn it. She was in need of a good rest and some peace. Back at home they would only be complaining again. She must know that it was in Anna's nature to act like that. If 'she' had complained in the maternity hospital, then 'she' would behave no differently at home. 'She' believed 'she' was the only female who knew everything and Ziggy had not forgotten how surprised 'she' was that things were working out for them – 'she' had hoped the young couple would end up with nothing.

Again Argentina was mentioned, and Ziggy asked Aiva to send a letter there to let Valdis and Ruta know they now had a daughter. She would also have to let others know about the birth. He wondered what her brother had to say about their having a daughter. And had her father been to visit, although he knew how difficult they made it for him to leave home to see her and the baby? In all honesty, things were not really that bad, but her mother had created a 'vipers' nest' in her head. Ziggy desired to get on with everyone and had managed not to crumple from their treatment of him. He would always be there to protect his new family and would no longer dance to their music. He suggested that Aiva's bad dreams were due to her worrying about everything.

Although Ziggy's health improved, he wasn't allowed to leave hospital. Other patients were now aware of his circumstances and loved the baby's name. Aiva had to register the birth and he told her to give all the names they had decided on. The certificate was to show Lolita Veronika Karolina Purins. He had written to Valdis and Ruta Briedis in Argentina and had enclosed Easter greetings from the three of them.

No letters had been kept from Aiva to Ziggy, except for just one she had written while in Priory Hospital. Today that hospital is known as St Thomas's. It was a workhouse until 1930. It became a hospital during the Second World War, and in 1978 it closed and was converted into flats. It was on the site of the excavated remains of an early thirteenth-century Augustinian priory, hence its name.

In her letter, Aiva said it was easier to write than to tell him in person how things were with her. That way Ziggy couldn't see her tears or hear her complaining. Lolita seemed to have inherited her nature and was a very content baby when with her. Everyone commented on what a beautiful baby she was. But she was not allowed to stay with her all the time, which may have been wise as the ward was draughty. Aiva was still not breastfeeding as it was decided by the medical staff that it could be a health risk to the baby; and if she was not producing enough milk, the baby would suffer.

Ziggy replied that he was overjoyed to have such a wonderful gift from Aiva, and words failed him. Their daughter was their life, and he was very pleased that they had a little girl. Perhaps they were meant to have a girl as they hadn't chosen any boys' names. Anna really didn't like them having a baby and didn't understand why they felt so fortunate. Ziggy could not comprehend that she would have been very happy if their daughter had not survived being born. He hated to be so blunt with Aiva, but those, he said, were the facts – words from her own mother's mouth. He thought Aiva would have been up and about after a week, but perhaps because she had lost quite a lot of blood she had to rest longer. He yearned to see his daughter. Life in hospital was boring. Every morning he longed for night-time. He thought the baby's snub nose was a mix of both their features, but they would see when she grew older whom she looked like the most. Ziggy had really hoped to be able to visit them on the Wednesday, and the matron knew how desperate he was to visit his wife and new baby.

However, on the Tuesday he received a letter saying Aiva had left the hospital. Ziggy had almost arranged a pointless journey to visit her and didn't understand her sudden exit for home. Had no one told her that she would be leaving hospital on Monday?

In a letter dated 15 April Ziggy asked Aiva how they were coping now they were back home. How was their health? Where did the baby sleep? He said she ought to buy a large basket to use as a temporary bed. There were more letters from Ziggy, always saying how lonely he was in hospital and wondering why Aiva didn't visit him, or at least write more often. Had they forgotten him? He couldn't think of an explanation. If she was fearful of the baby catching a disease from the hospital, she could hold the baby up to the window to show him how she was developing. Another patient had his wife do that. He continued to worry about their health and how things were at home. (Sadness oozed from between the lines.)

On 7 May the doctor was going to put a big needle in Ziggy's chest to test for possible fluid. However, as his examination showed good progress with his lungs they postponed the procedure. Ziggy had put on fourteen pounds in weight while in hospital. He was allowed to walk around for a couple of hours, and he imagined he would be heading for home in about three weeks' time. However, a week later the doctor decided he should carry out the procedure and two fat needles were inserted through his ribcage. This was necessary to make sure there was no fluid between his lungs and his ribs. The needles went into the suspicious areas on the left side, which made Ziggy feel terrible and start to sweat. This was made worse by the process being so slow. The sister and matron held him and tried to be reassuring so that he didn't faint. No liquid was found. Not satisfied, the doctor repeated this on the other side. Ziggy was now sweating profusely and did not think he could tolerate any more. The matron then brought him a generous glass of cognac to help him cope with the torturous second needle. But there was no fluid on that side either. He felt much happier afterwards as he would no longer need to rest and would hopefully be home in a couple of weeks' time. The matron and doctor assured him that his lungs would be fine, and he had to have bed rest to allow the needle punctures to heal. The diagnosis of pleurisy had first been suggested in Germany. However, the doctors also insisted that he did not have tuberculosis and had never had it in the past.

Again Ziggy complained that Aiva's letters were vague. He wanted to know exactly what was the matter. Had there been a falling-out with those at home? Or had there been bad news? As she had mentioned having to pull herself together, there must have been a crisis. He asked her to please tell him as their problems should be shared. He also queried why she had changed her mind over the baby's names and had decided against Veronika. She was never to think that he felt anger towards her. What he did feel was heartache as things were not how they should be. If only the situation at home was better. If they all helped each other, then he would have no need to worry. He fretted that Anna was trying to persuade Aiva to leave him and was trying to alienate him. He knew that Aiva's mother could be very scheming and wouldn't think twice about upsetting others to get her own way. It was hopeless when there was no peace and harmony in a family, especially when there were so many difficulties to face. They could only hope that there would be some respite, and all would be well in the end.

Had any work being carried out on the boat in his absence?

What exactly had been done and had they managed to sell the scrap metal?

Ziggy's other worry always seemed to be about his laundry. He never had clean pyjamas and socks, and his wife didn't appear to have the time to provide him with those. He complained he had to wash his own socks at night and he couldn't repair the holes. Surely someone else could visit him with essentials? He had no family visiting him the whole time he was there, which made fellow patients realise that not all was well in his home.

They were reliant on benefit payments, which amounted to very little. However, he thought one payment would be enough for them to buy a pram. He insisted they must not have a second-hand one. Although he didn't know how much a new one would cost, he thought they might be able to buy one for around £10. Aiva must have commented at some point that he didn't take life seriously enough as he insisted that he might be smiling on the outside, but inside he was shedding bitter tears. All would be better when their little family lived separately from Aiva's parents. All he desired was peaceful harmony.

On 20 May he still complained about what was happening to them. In all his twenty-eight years he had never experienced so many raised voices, so many lies and so much ill will as had happened during the last summer and autumn. And that would continue if they carried on living with her parents. If only he could let it all go over his head, but as he was so sensitive it affected him badly. Aiva had chosen him to be her soulmate, and now he worried that she was being turned against him. He realised that no other woman would have put up with all she had to tolerate because of him. He tried to open up his heart to her and hope she wouldn't feel resentment towards him for doing that.

The doctors did not allow Ziggy to leave hospital just yet, but he pleaded with them to allow him to visit his family. It was against hospital rules to allow any patients out unless it was an emergency. This would be his last outing, and if nothing untoward happened, he would be seeing his wife and daughter on the following Saturday.

Ziggy and Aiva on board the Tobago.

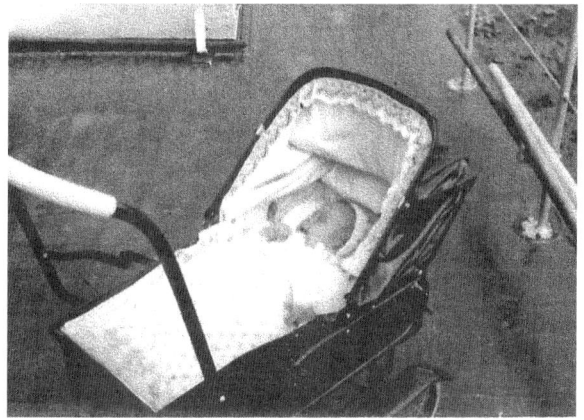

Baby Lolita at approximately eight weeks old. Aiva had crocheted her outfit and blanket.

On 31 May Ziggy commented in his letter that the two days he had spent with his wife and baby had gone by so quickly it had felt like a moment. It had been difficult parting again as he knew it would be another three weeks before he would see them again. Aiva had cried when he departed, and he hoped that the next time they were together he would never ever have to leave her. He longed for the day when he would be able to leave that place and go home permanently. There was nowhere in the world he would rather be than with his wife and daughter. Their biggest purpose in life would be to rear their little one, to care for her, and to never give their children the terrible heartache that they had had to suffer.

Their aim would be to have independence, and never to have to rely on others. In the following year their lives might be uncertain, but would be more stable. Ziggy wished for God's help and advice to overcome their financial problems.

Rolands was still around, working on the boat. He had been trying to deal with wood materials and a broken saw. There was also still the desire for them to leave Britain in the summer with their boat. Ziggy believed that their daughter would be strong enough and would come to no harm during the journey. Children are usually quite robust. He was very happy that after all the problems Aiva had experienced during pregnancy, she had given birth to such a healthy baby. Also, he thought Aiva should be able to tolerate a long voyage. They would need good weather for the journey across the Bay of Biscay. But perhaps they ought to sail straight across the Atlantic? All they needed was enough money to fill the boat up with fuel. They could then head for the sun.

Ziggy's very last letter from the hospital was dated 12 June, and in it he confirmed the great news that he would be on his way home on Saturday between 4 p.m. and 5 p.m. He hoped that Aiva liked his news. He was pushed for time as he had started a craftwork project and needed to complete it in time for his going home. He understood if her hands were full with the baby and if she had no time for her 'old man'. Hopefully, that situation would improve when they were together again. But they must all understand that he wouldn't be able to carry out any heavy work as his muscles had wasted away after five months in hospital. If he pushed himself too much, he could end up in a bad way again.

What is not understood is why the medical staff were not honest with the family about Ziggy's state of health. Why was he allowed to leave the hospital? There was a report from the Public Health Laboratory Service in Carmarthen with the results of his sputum test carried out in Sealyham Hospital. Dated 19 March 1952, it said that after six weeks the culture showed a 'growth of colonies of acid-fast bacilli, identical with *Mycobacterium tuberculosis*'. There were also two sick notes from Dr P. D. Gange in Milford Haven certifying that Zigfrids Heinrichs Purins had been unfit for work since September 1951 on account of pulmonary tuberculosis, which is contagious. It can be spread from person to person through the air. It usually affects the lungs and is curable with the right treatment and with antibiotics. Pleurisy is inflammation of the pleura, which is the tissue lining the lungs and chest cavity, and can be caused by a lung infection such as tuberculosis.

From 1952 to 1956 Ziggy was registered as disabled and classed himself as self-employed as he was converting the E-boat into a houseboat as well as an ocean-going vessel.

Lolita celebrating her first Christmas in the dining area of the Tobago, *1952. (Left to right, Ziggy, Janis, Aiva, Anna and Rolands.)*

Ziggy and Aiva rented two furnished rooms and a shared kitchenette from 21 February until 30 October 1954. They lived at 10 Greville Road, Milford Haven, which cost them £2 per week. As work was still being carried out on the boat, they continued to spend some of their time on her. Their next move was to 28 Stratford Road, also in Milford Haven. Then from 19 August until 23 December 1956 Aiva and Ziggy lived with the Webb family at 62 Priory Road.

During this period Ziggy had been exchanging letters with a lady called E. Krumins. On 21 April 1954 there was a letter from her in Canada, where she lived on 2037 Harold Street in the Niagara Falls area of Ontario. She thanked him for his letter and lovely photo. She was very happy to hear that he had come to his senses and had made the decision to move to Canada. It was a land of opportunity for young people. Had they applied for the necessary documents? She would help them as much as she could, so he should not be afraid to ask. She was longing to see them.

Lolita could go and live with her while Aiva and Ziggy worked and earned the necessary dollars. In their photo they looked like an attractive couple, meant for each other, she said.

In June 1956 Ziggy was issued with another Disabled Persons Certificate, valid until June 1958.

It was decided that Ziggy would move to Cardiff to attend the motor-vehicle course at Llandaff Technical College. He won a prize for his studies and qualified in March 1957. He rented a room at 94 Miskin Street, Cathays, and while living there he looked for suitable accommodation for his wife and child. As part of his training he was also employed and earned £5 18s. per week and had an accommodation allowance of £2 5s.; but on moving, he would lose that. He sent Aiva lots of love and many kisses in affectionate letters. He told her he was friendly with a couple called Olga and Sasha, who had offered a lot of advice on the best way to find a suitable flat, and he advised her to slowly start packing. It seemed that he could easily get them a flat which would cost forty-five to fifty shillings per week. Olga would put an advert in the paper on their behalf. Ziggy said he would see Aiva in a week's time and then they would travel to Cardiff together. The area he lived in was not particularly good and he wouldn't like them to all live there if they had a choice. Then in his next letter he told her to pack as quickly as she could because on Friday or Saturday a big van would turn up. Olga had organised it as the company she worked for was based in Milford Haven. Even if everything fell through with the potential flat, they could live with Sasha, who had plenty of space. Ziggy would be on the 9.45 p.m. train home to her on Thursday.

Aiva replied by saying that although it was generous of Sasha and Olga to offer them a temporary home, Ziggy knew that she was not one to hang on to anyone's neck, and she was still too tired to socialise. Also, she could never feel settled until they had moved into their own place. If all their clothes were packed up, it would be awkward to get dressed properly; and if they were in someone else's house, they would feel like visitors. Also, they would not be able to have a proper relationship. She would rather wait another week if necessary. Aiva tried to reassure him by saying he was not to think that she didn't want to rush to be by his side, but she would rather Ziggy took his time and found them somewhere nice to live. Meanwhile, she would start sorting out their belongings and would pack up what they could manage without. How would they manage on the fifty shillings benefit they would have if he only studied and didn't work? Ziggy was only to make the journey if he found rooms for them, as they could not afford to waste money on fares. She said she could continue her letter by telling him about the boat and about the gearbox, but the laundry had to be done before her mother decided to come and help her. The boat could not be moved from Milford Haven until Rolands managed to buy a cheap gearbox. The boat also needed to be painted properly. Aiva also tried to assure him that as the weather had been warm, there had been no need to light the fire. That meant she had spare coal, so he was not to worry about them keeping warm. She also advised Ziggy to negotiate any rent as every shilling they saved was worth having. It was doubtful that they could get a separate bedroom for little Lolly, but she told him at least to make sure their bedroom was quite spacious and that a school wasn't far away. He then had to check that it wasn't noisy as there could be a lodger in the building doing shift work. Their rooms must also be airy and dry. Lolita was well and not one day passed when she didn't mention her daddy, and she sent him an armful of kisses, counting them as well as she could. Aiva ended her letter with loving and sincere kisses from her to him.

Ziggy's regular routine was to get up at 6.45 a.m. and to leave for college at 7.35 a.m. He travelled by bus, then walked. He started at 8 a.m. and finished at 5 p.m. He would then rush back for his evening meal, which, although adequate, was not tasty. Any spare money left after his expenses he would send to Aiva. He told her that she had no idea just how much he missed her and how much he longed to hold her and love her. . . . He wondered if her family were trying to dissuade her from going to Cardiff.

No diaries or letters exist relating to Lolita's early years. While still living in Milford Haven she had a vivid imagination and decided that stones from the garden could be used as money.

She once got as far as the bus stop before Aiva managed to catch up with her and stopped her boarding the bus. Behind their house was a huge field and the fair used to arrive there once a year. They kept chickens in the garden for their eggs. Ziggy had brought them home one Christmas, alive in a sack, for dinner, but no one had the heart to kill them. So the chickens had a happy life, but they liked to escape into the neighbours' gardens and Lolita used to chase them and try and bring them home. Two doors away lived Lolita's friend Linda, whose father owned a butcher's shop. She was three years older. Lolita would visit her on her tricycle as she liked to look at the collection of teddy bears kept in the outside lavatory. From her swing, Lolita could see into Linda's garden. The only problem was that sometimes Linda wouldn't allow her to go home and she was too small to reach the garden gate latch. Then Aiva would scold her for being late, which felt really unfair. Near home there was an open-air swimming pool, but Lolita didn't have a proper swimsuit. She wasn't keen on paddling. Aiva could see nothing wrong in Lolita wearing just panties, but she was very self-conscious. Apparently she had many little friends – too many to come into the house at the same time. She was only allowed one friend at a time to come in and play.

Lolita was a little rebel. She was always warned not to touch the oven knobs, but she would keep twiddling them when she thought no one was looking. One day, with her back against the oven, she managed to tip a saucepan of boiling water over her foot. She could remember her mother rushing around and Granny coming to visit. As she couldn't walk on her foot, she sat in her old pram eating an orange. Unfortunately, she was left with a scar on her foot, though it did fade gradually with age.

When the time came to leave Milford Haven, Janis, Anna and Rolands sailed to Cardiff in their boat. Lolita and Aiva travelled by what looked huge to a small child, a steam train.

In 1957 the boat was moored in West Bute Dock, Tiger Bay, Cardiff. The inspiration for the name *Tobago* was that Latvia in the seventeenth century was the smallest nation to have colonial power. The tribes set up colonies in Tobago, and were excellent sailors.

From December 1956 to October 1957 Aiva, Ziggy and Lolita lived in 67 Westville Road, opposite Waterloo Road Park in Cardiff. The rooms were rented from a Mrs Sprunks, who was rather an unpleasant landlady. She gave the little girl graphic war magazines, and wasn't kind. Aiva didn't like her child looking at such magazines and would take them off her. Aiva worked hard there, doing all the housework in part exchange for rent.

Anna and Janis having a farewell party on the MV Tobago *before leaving Milford Haven.*

Rolands and Janis sailing to Cardiff.

After Ziggy qualified in March 1957, he started working for Syd S. Jones of Albany Road. He was employed as a mechanic, working very long hours. One week he did as many as sixty-five hours. Luck was not on his side, and on 26 August 1957 he was yet again admitted into hospital. This time he was a patient in Powys Ward E of Sully Hospital.

In November 1936 Sully Hospital opened for the diagnosis, treatment and prevention of tuberculosis, in the village of Sully, seven miles from Cardiff. It was sited in extensive wooded grounds between Barry and Penarth. During the Second World War it began to admit non-tuberculosis patients and served as a general chest and heart treatment facility. In 2001 it closed as an NHS hospital, and as it was a listed building it was converted into luxury apartments and renamed Hayes Point.

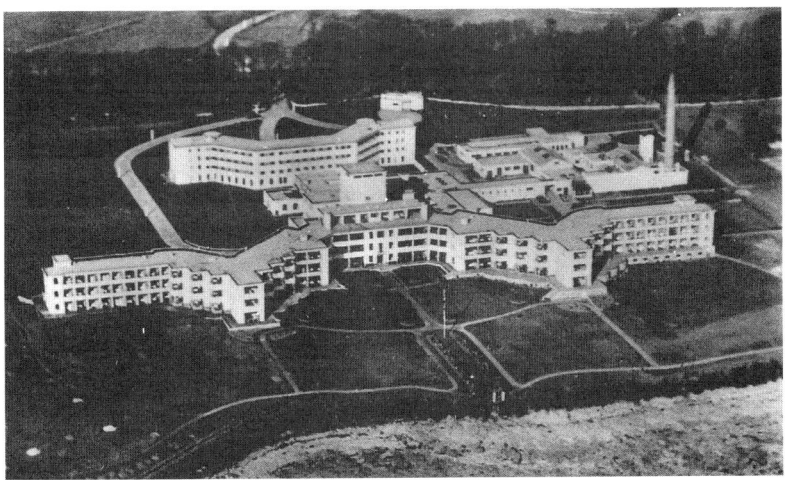

Sully Hospital, Sully, Glamorgan.

In the 1950s abortion was illegal, secret, scary and also expensive. The unpleasant procedure involved a metal rod being inserted and remaining in position for twenty-four hours. The uterus would contract in response to the intrusion of the foreign object. Then a sharp-edged metal loop was used to scrape away the lining. Septic shock sometimes caused the organs to fail and the girls died. However, if you were living in poverty and could only find an illegal set-up in the dingy backstreets of Tiger Bay, then you were dealt with in a very basic manner with a wire coat hanger. The chances of the woman having another baby were, sadly, remote. Ziggy, in desperation, helped his wife down that route. It was never spoken about. But I never had any siblings, for which Aiva always felt deep regret.

Back in hospital, Ziggy would gravitate towards anyone from the Baltic States. Elgate, known by everyone as Helga, worked as a tuberculosis nurse in Sully. Ziggy struck up a friendship with her as she was a nurse on his ward. Helga was Estonian and had met her Latvian husband, Alfons Kudins, in Düsseldorf Displaced Persons Camp. He was in the Latvian Legion and she was a children's nurse. When they came to Britain for employment, they settled in Cardiff. Alfons worked on a farm in Thornhill, Cardiff, then trained as a nurse. Through Helga, Ziggy got to know Alfons, who became a great help in enabling Aiva to visit Ziggy, as she had no available transport otherwise.

Again there was a pile of letters from Ziggy to his wife. He spent his birthday in the September confined to hospital. While he was away, Mrs Sprunks decided she would evict Aiva with Lolita. She wrongly and ridiculously accused Aiva of going out at all hours, of having gentlemen callers, and getting together with Mr Kudins, who was not welcome because of his 'reputation'. Alfons would defend himself and told Ziggy that as he would otherwise be sitting alone at home, or would be down the pub, he was happy to give Aiva lifts to the hospital. When he took his children, Leon, Karina and Andrea, to the seaside, he kindly took Lolita with them. Ziggy was furious with Mrs Sprunks and wrote to her, accusing her of doing 'Devil's work' and said she behaved in a non-Christian manner, especially as they were experiencing difficult times, and his wife had been of great help to her. He added that Mrs Sprunks didn't have a good word to say about anybody – not even her own son.

In Lolita's eyes, Mrs Sprunks was a really overweight lady who never allowed her to touch any of her ornaments even though she never tried to actually pick one up. However, there was a very nice lady who lived next door, made friends with the little girl and allowed her into her home. She would lift Lolita up to show her the glass ornaments on the mantelpiece. In return, Lolita would cut out cartoon strips from the newspaper and hand them to her when she was out mowing the lawn.

In the October, Aiva received a letter from another Latvian lady, Rasma Spalvainis, who expressed her shock that they had been given notice to leave their rooms. If needed, she could help them out and she said Lolita had to be considered because of having to attend school.

It seemed that every time Ziggy was in hospital Aiva found excuses not to visit him. She made out he was being unreasonable as he expected her to catch buses and risk illness from being out in the cold and damp weather. But he was obviously not keen on Mr Kudins giving her lifts so often, as he really wished for some private time with her. Ziggy felt he was incarcerated. His enforced stay in hospital was very boring and he told Aiva he missed her company. Aiva would respond by saying that she also felt imprisoned, in their little flat. Therefore she felt gratitude if she was taken to the cinema and didn't have to pay. Ziggy always seemed caring and used to ask how little Lolita was, how she was progressing, and was she going to school? But Aiva would only reply that Lolita sent her kisses to him. He believed he would be home within a couple of weeks, but the doctors informed him that there was still fluid in his chest. If they couldn't draw it out with needles it could mean an operation, but that seemed unlikely.

Aiva was desperate to get away from living with the unpleasant and unreasonable Mrs Sprunks, but finding another flat was easier said than done. An example of her behaviour was that when there was a power cut Aiva couldn't carry out the required chores. The cleaning was done in exchange for rent reduction. If there was no electricity, then there was no hot water. Aiva couldn't clean without hot water, so her rent went up, even though she didn't have any hot water for her own use. Friends always knew of a 'suitable' flat for her, but not many landlords were willing to accept a young child or risk a woman with an absent husband, even though he was hospitalised. Life became intolerable for her. Ziggy tried to be reassuring by telling her to live in hope and that life would run more smoothly for them soon.

Fortunately, by the end of October 1957 Aiva had been offered a temporary respite by a Mrs Eglitis, a very pleasant Estonian lady who had rooms in 22 Kingsland Road in the Canton area of Cardiff. Aiva did her best to settle in with Lolita; Ziggy could only remain in the background while she faced problems and upheaval on her own.

Ziggy discovered that he had some talent as an artist when he started to paint for the first time as part of his occupational therapy in hospital. His landscapes were selling for £2 each, which was a good amount at the time.

In his letter of 4 November, Ziggy asked why when Aiva visited were her thoughts elsewhere? She seemed more nervous and unhappy – not like other times. Was she feeling depressed? After all, things were not really that bad, and life would improve for them. He claimed his health was on the mend, and that the nurses seemed hopeful about his recovery. His next letter contained an air of optimism as the needles were successfully removing the fluid, and that made him feel less miserable.

Ziggy received sickness benefit from the Ministry of Pensions and National Insurance, and he was reminded that his medical certificate would expire on 24/02/1958 and had to be renewed for his benefit to continue.

Then the doctors decided that Ziggy's condition was worse than they had previously thought, and an operation was needed after all. With a diagram he tried to illustrate to Aiva where the pocket of fluid was that had to be removed from his chest. Unfortunately, there was a thickened wall between the fluid and his lung. If that didn't shrink after the fluid was drained, it could be life-threatening if left. He could be given special medication to soften that wall, but then he would be confined to bed rest for a month, with no guarantee it would work. The quickest solution would be to operate in a few weeks' time.

During this time, Aiva unsuccessfully tried to find another, more permanent, flat for them. Then she fretted that she was becoming old and ugly, although she was only twenty-nine years old. Ziggy tried to reassure her and said that in his eyes she would always be young and beautiful. Everyone grows older, and he hadn't married her just because of her beauty. He loved her. If she remained in love with him, then they could tolerate any obstacles life threw at them and they would overcome anything. His dearest wish was for Aiva to be happy. Ziggy couldn't wait for her visits as they were the highlight of his week.

The concern over having no real place of their own to live in continued. Ziggy's operation was due at the beginning of December. A 'bronchogram' had been carried out. That involved pumping white liquid into his lungs, which he then had to cough out over the next couple of days. He hadn't found the process too awful, but some patients said they would rather throw themselves out of the window than go through it again. He had reacted to the treatment by having the shakes and a high temperature. He now felt better and his temperature had lowered. The doctors stressed that this was normal. Ziggy was then allowed to go home for a week before the operation was carried out.

When he returned to the ward there had been changes. Ziggy's bed had been moved to a different position, and new patients had been admitted. A number of operations had been carried out successfully. He didn't sleep well and felt so lonely he could cry.

There was no way Aiva could imagine his contentment when she was lying next to him. If he woke up, he could feel her closeness. That made him feel so wonderful that he was able to fall asleep again. There was nothing he would have loved more than to put all his belongings in a bag and hotfoot it back to his dear wife. If the operation took place the following week, he would be able to head for home in a couple of months' time.

But no operation took place on 3 December, though it had been promised. Instead a plaster cast was made of his torso and it would have to be worn in bed after they decided to operate. Could Aiva bring him some money as he had basketwork to do? He was about to make a waste-paper basket and two fruit baskets, and needed five shillings to buy the necessary materials. When they were sold, he would get his money back. He was also owed thirteen shillings for two trays and a picnic basket he had already made. The two trays were an order which had yet to be collected by a young man. Ziggy wanted to complete all the work as he hoped the operation would at last be carried out the following week.

Ziggy was concerned about Aiva's safety when she walked to

visit their boat in the docks. She had joked about being followed, but he scolded her for making light of it. She really shouldn't walk alone in the dark, especially between the two railway sheds, he told her. He realised that she didn't have much choice until they had a proper home. He would feel much happier when she had moved in with the Spalvainis family as they had a pleasant home and were decent people. Aiva, however, criticised him and accused him of not being 'streetwise' as he was a country lad with a narrow outlook on life. His response was to say that he tried to do all he could for her, and it was done from pure love for her. If she knew him better, she would be more understanding, and would not be so sensitive, he said. All he desired was her happiness, and a bright future for them. Would she be patient and wait for him to come home? Or would she find love with someone else? If only they could have had their own little house, as then things would have been very different. Instead she had to aimlessly wander around and face problems on her own. Ziggy felt he was not good enough for her as he couldn't give them a normal life, although he aimed to do that to the best of his ability.

On 10 December Ziggy was moved to a private ward, which had the letter 'L' on the door. The doctors discussed his operation, which would take place on the Friday. He felt some relief that things would happen at last, as he hated the not knowing. Perhaps if Mr Kudins was able to come, and she was available, they could visit on the Thursday? Aiva told him not to worry so much, to which he replied by saying that to not worry would mean he didn't care. And he loved her with all his heart.

An exhibition was to take place on Saturday and Sunday showing the patients' craftwork, which included his own. He had nearly finished a painting which everyone complimented him on, and it would be on display. It was of a waterside with an elevated castle. Awards would be given, and he hoped that he would win at least one prize. Nobody believed that he hadn't been to art college and was totally ignorant about art.

On Thursday 12 December the staff prepared Ziggy for theatre at 9.30 a.m. He was given penicillin injections, then a sedative.

On 13 December a student nurse wrote to Aiva on Ziggy's behalf as he couldn't physically put pen to paper. He'd had his operation and was 'progressing slowly, because his operation was pretty big'.

Ziggy was unable to write any letters until 16 December as he hadn't been able to sit up. He would be kept in the post-op area until the tubes were removed. They would then move him to a ward downstairs. He was feeling stronger. Aiva had not visited him as she had claimed to have flu and said she might end up spending Christmas in bed, which seemed sad. . . .

On 17 December, just after 7 a.m., Ziggy was allowed to sit up long enough to write a letter. Other than at mealtimes, he had to remain lying down. This would have to continue for ten days, until the stitches were removed. Then he would be able to remain sitting up in bed except for periods of sleep. He was given details of his operation, which had lasted two and a half hours and had gone well. His progress was good. Usually the tubes were removed after six days, but his came out after only three days. He said he would go into more detail when he saw Aiva again. His swollen hands were better, and as he had been given painkillers he wasn't in discomfort. He had also been given three pints of blood and two pints of plasma.

Ziggy wrote on 20 December expressing how very happy he felt that Aiva had managed to visit him, as he had been longing to see her. Although she'd had flu, he thought she looked well. With Christmas in mind, he told her whom she should send cards to and buy presents for. In the way he expressed himself he comes across as a kind and considerate man.

His next letter was written after Christmas. Ziggy wished with all his heart that his dearest wife would have a very happy and love-filled New Year, and that 1958 would be a much better year than the last. She was to wish little Lolita all the best in life, with lots of love from him. Her letter to him cheered him up. If she thought another flat was possible for them in Albany Road, then that would be much better for them. The houses were good and it would be nearer to work for him. It would be nearer to school for the little one as well. If Aiva was busy arranging a move, she should not visit him as a new place to live was far more important. Ziggy had never imagined just how weak the operation would leave him. Although he looked well, he had no idea where his strength had gone – a real mystery to him.

A week later, Aiva visited and managed to upset him. To her it seemed that he was not looking after his health properly, and wasn't eating enough. He felt that she could only understand if she was in his place. She mustn't forget that he had been through quite a serious operation, which could cause complications, he told her. Ziggy had a temperature and the medication made his appetite disappear. Neither the nurses nor the doctors could give him any reason for his setback. He was also unhappy that the house move had not taken place as he had hoped. And his heart was heavy as Aiva had not written to him.

Ziggy had felt lonely and abandoned until her visit the previous evening. It wasn't often they could discuss personal matters, especially as some stranger was likely to be nearby and then he couldn't feel free with her. At least they were able to chat for forty-five minutes, which reassured and calmed him. He had been given two bottles of Guinness beer, which he should try and drink, even if he didn't fancy them. He would have enjoyed the beer if he was with Aiva, but on his own he didn't want them.

On 10 January 1958 Ziggy wrote to Aiva saying that he felt much better. His extreme tiredness had gone and he was eating like a horse. The ward sister said his weight of eleven stone nine pounds was OK, but he mustn't put on too much as that wouldn't be good for him. As his temperature was down and he was sleeping well he felt much brighter. He was now allowed to take a walk a couple of times a day. He continued to worry about Aiva – that she was doing too much – and he told her she must not overdo things. She must take life slowly, especially with a possible move. She mustn't become weak as she was the only joy in the world to him.

By 14 January Ziggy was allowed to get up and go and wash himself. The doctors just smiled and said very little. Not much had changed. He just wished the time would pass more quickly so that he could go home and share all of Aiva's highs and lows. He wondered if there was any point in them continuing to look elsewhere to live as they couldn't find any rooms that would be suitable. As they had failed, perhaps Aiva could think about seeing if it would be possible for them to remain there? He was relieved to hear that she had managed to light the fire and wouldn't freeze.

Maybe she ought to buy some coal? Or maybe she could offer the landlady more rent to cover the cost of the fuel? That way she would always be warm through the worst of the winter.

On 19 January Ziggy again longed for Aiva to come alone when visiting, and pleaded for her to do so at least once. Did she no longer want to be alone with him? For a couple of weeks yet the doctors wouldn't be telling him when he might be allowed home. He said she couldn't possibly imagine how much he wanted to get out of there. His greatest fear was that something would prevent him leaving the hospital. The most popular topic of conversation among the patients was about going home. If Aiva had married someone else, she might not have had to face so many difficulties and her life might have been much happier. He ordered her to dress warmly and to keep the fire lit as he didn't want her to catch a cold. Then he worried that perhaps she misunderstood him, which was why he needed to spend more time with her. He told her she must realise that if she left him, he would surely end up remaining in Sully. Aiva would then be free to say and think whatever she liked. But then, without her, his own life would have no meaning.

Ziggy's letter on 23 January said that it was cold and snowing heavily. At that rate he thought it would be two feet deep by night-time. Hopefully the roads wouldn't become blocked; otherwise he wouldn't be seeing her on Sunday. It would be better if she stayed at home, in the warm, as she wasn't strong. He thought he would be allowed home by the end of February, if not sooner. He was sorry if he upset her, but he felt heavy-hearted while in hospital. There were times he was overwhelmed by his longing for her, and he tried to imagine he was somewhere else.

In the morning of 28 January he enjoyed some Scotch porridge oats before he tucked into his proper breakfast of sausages and fried tomatoes. The weather looked awful – there were strong winds and heavy rain. Aiva had been to visit on the Sunday and they had discussed another possible flat that had become available. But he wasn't keen as he had heard that the landlady was aggressive and jealous, and you never knew when her bad moods would be aimed at you. Ziggy's lessons had been continuing well, but as his English wasn't very good he had to ask for help at times to understand problems that needed solving. He hoped Aiva's X-rays had gone well as he knew she had been worrying about them. As the doctors had told her that the shadow on her lungs had disappeared, and her weight was stable, she should have had no need to keep worrying.

The weather had been springlike, so he wrote on 30 January to say he had been allowed to have a stroll outside. He had worn her gift of the cardigan, which fitted him like a glove. It was easy to put on quickly and he was really grateful. He was sure that being more active made him feel much better. Aiva had written to tell him that Rolands was contemplating sailing to the island of Tobago. He had read somewhere that it was very colourful and offered good living. But you had to be employed. He would move there with his parents; and if all went well, there would be no reason why they couldn't join him with their boat. He had also heard that those who had gone there to be fishermen hadn't come back as there was no shortage of fish to supply the factories with. Anyway, they would have plenty of time to discuss it all further when Ziggy was home again.

By 8 February he was slowly getting stronger and felt quite well. He would be asking the doctor if he could go home on the 21st. He was short of money again as he had to buy more kits for commissions for his trays. He also wrote that the ward had visitors from the Seaman's Club. The ladies had brought them Christmas cake, fruit, and two jars of jam each. He wondered if Aiva had been to the cinema recently? He told her when he was out and back in his stride they would go to all sorts of places and make up for lost time. He asked how Rolands had got on in Liverpool. Also, he thought that if they remained living at Mrs Eglitis's the little one should go to school as she was nearly six years of age!

On 11 February Ziggy had an update on his health. The doctors were saying his last X-ray showed all was well and that there was no reason for him to remain in hospital. So he was going home on Friday, the following week. He was going home where he belonged, and where Aiva and Lolita were waiting for him. Now, not only was he allowed to exercise more, but he could also have his lunch in the dining room. And he no longer had to stay in bed during visiting time. He was ecstatic at the thought of being able to return to normal family life, and impatiently waited for the ten days to pass – the sooner the better to leave the hospital 'atmosphere'. And he hoped that she was feeling healthy and bright, and was waiting impatiently for him to come home.

A couple of days later Aiva wrote to say that in the house the German lodger was leaving her flat, and they could take it over. Ziggy told her to ask how much rent was being asked and felt they should offer to pay £2 as they wouldn't get anything better or cheaper. Could she please take some of his belongings home when she visited on Sunday, so that he would have less to carry when he left? He also wanted a clean vest to put on after he'd had a bath before leaving. Every day he had been going outside to get used to the fresh air. Also, he had to finish a painting for which he would be paid £3. He couldn't wait for them to lead normal lives at long last. Ziggy also hoped that those on the boat didn't expect him to do any labour on it while he was off work. He really didn't think his body would tolerate it, besides which he had no desire to go there.

Ziggy's next letter from Aiva told him that they hadn't, as yet, moved over to the other flat as it was being decorated. Any increase in rent would be discussed when he was home again. Every day she had visited the boat, but today she would do all the ironing, then have a bath and wash her hair. She wanted to be nice and clean for his homecoming. Lolita was very happy, perhaps because she thought he would bring her something. Their bedroom hadn't been heated as she wanted to save the coal for when he came home, as he wouldn't be used to sleeping in a cold room. She prayed that this would be the last time they were so mercilessly parted.

On 22 February Ziggy wrote his last letter to Aiva from Sully. He would be leaving the hospital at 9.45 a.m., and would arrive in Cardiff around 10.20 a.m. Unfortunately he hadn't found anything he thought suitable to buy Lolita. His hospital paperwork was already in his pocket. Everything was OK.

My parents paid rent of £2 5s. for the two furnished rooms per week.

I can recall my father coming out of hospital with a huge scar down his back from the operation. I only have a few childhood memories from that time in February 1958 and they don't include any periods of unhappiness. A treat for me would be to have an ice cream or lollipop from a shop down the main road. I loved to go to Victoria Park and thoroughly enjoyed the swings, slide, roundabout, and being in the sandpit beneath the trees. Also, I liked to paddle in the pool, which had a fountain in the centre. Our neighbours on one side were very noisy. They were always shouting and we had to turn up the volume on the radio so as not to hear them. I was friendly with their little girl, who was a bit grubby. However, the other people who lived in that house were a decent family and used to give me biscuits to take home, and offered their help if needed. I used to walk to school with the little girl; but she was always late, which made me late too. As a punishment we ended up having to stand in front of the class with our backs turned to them. We were pupils in Lansdowne Road Infant School, and I quite enjoyed being at that school. When we had art class, we would play shops and families. The headmistress quite liked me and would let me help her with the decorations at Christmas. There was also a wigwam made out of sheets of paper, and we took turns to sit inside it on a cushion, for a day, eating peanuts. We would read books of Red Indian stories.

Mrs Eglitis bought me a pretty dress for my sixth birthday, and I was also given a doll with long blonde hair I could style and plait. I also have a vague memory of carrying glass milk bottles – I fell with them and cut my cheek, leaving me with a slight scar. I was so ill from measles there that I was allowed to sleep in my parents' comfortable double bed with the curtains drawn closed to prevent my eyes from hurting from the light. Mother would read to me and feed me. Lucozade was the cure-all in those days!

I had a young friend called Albert Jaksts, who was quite a little gentleman, especially in his bow tie. He would play with my dolls as well as playing cowboys and Indians with me. He sent me a Robinson's golliwog brooch, which seemed a special gift. When he left for Canada he gave me a lot of his possessions, including a world globe. When my mother was ill, I would make her sandwiches, and my friends used to come and watch, amazed by how clever I was! Their parents would comment to mine that their children would go home and speak very strangely. They were then informed, as Latvian was my first language, that they had learned a lot of words from me!

We didn't have a television, so I used to sit at the bottom of the stairs and wait for Mrs Eglitis to come out of her front room and invite me in to watch her television. One time I had the bright idea of trying to roll down the stairs, one step at a time. But when I tried, I rolled all the way down and yelled my head off at the bottom. My mother panicked, thinking I had killed myself. But I was unhurt. Another lady lived in the same house. She was kind, and very patient with me. I used to watch her knit and ask to have a go. But I would just tangle it all up. In the end, she taught me to knit properly, the continental way. Next door there was an elderly lady who gave me home-made cakes and played games with me. We played I spy, and named animals in a zoo with each letter of the alphabet. A present from her was a jointed wooden black cat with a bell around its neck.

Unfortunately, we had to move again as Mrs Eglitis wanted to decorate our rooms and use them for herself. I had just started the first class in junior school. I enjoyed rainy days as then we were allowed to stay indoors and read comics during break times. Because I was leaving I was allowed an extra bottle of the free milk we used to have daily, and I could visit the school library.

Mrs Eglitis felt she ought to apologise to us for forcing us to move. As a farewell present she gave me a mechanical tin monkey on a string, which, when tugged, made the monkey climb the string. And the kind lady who also lived there gave me a solid-silver bracelet which she no longer wanted.

My father was now earning a regular wage, and fortunately he found a house we could move to. There was an elegant terraced Victorian house for sale on Kimberley Road, Penylan. We could move into our new home, number 30, whenever it suited us. How wonderful to have a whole house to ourselves! As you entered the tiled hallway, the front parlour for guests and special occasions was to the left. Then you entered the family living room. Down some steps was the kitchen with an open range fireplace and walk-in pantry. As it used to be the servants' quarters, there were bells on the wall indicating which room needed service. Back up the steps, you went upstairs to a separate toilet and bathroom on a landing. Then up more stairs were three bedrooms – two at the front and one at the back of the house. The last flight of stairs led to just one bedroom, which was mine. It overlooked the back garden with a garage at the bottom, which was entered via the back lane. There was also a cellar with a coal chute.

In June 1958 Sully Hospital sent Father an appointment for him to attend their X-ray department in Cardiff Royal Infirmary in September. He then needed another X-ray on 28 January 1959, which resulted in his being hospitalised from 11 February until the 15th.

During this time, my great-grandmother Kristine Mikelsons decided to get in touch and was writing letters to her family in Britain and in Australia. Kristine was born on 20 January 1874 and her home was Krisjan Baron Road 39, Flat 24, Riga. In one letter, dated 18 September 1957, she wrote to 'her dearest children', and sent her sincere best wishes to them. She longed for them all to write more often as she had only had two letters. Could Rolands and his father write about their health? And had Rolands really not found himself a young lady? Her daughter, Alida, had written to her from Australia, and she was happy to hear what a caring mother she was with her own children. It was a pity that they didn't live together, but it was a relief that Alida had managed to locate her family when she originally had no idea where they were. They really must communicate more often and not live like strangers, she said. Kristine had been to visit Zigfrids' mother, Milda. She managed to stay a whole week with her in the Sigulda area, and she said Milda was very sweet and lovely. Milda loved her company and wished she would stay with her through the winter as she wasn't happy on her own. But Kristine was caught up with all her chores and with beekeeping, so she didn't have time to travel and visit. Milda's house was tidy, but the barn needed a new roof. Kristine promised to help her out by sending her money, and by taking her a few essentials. Aiva had asked her grandmother for an amber necklace, but Kristine didn't think she would be allowed to mail her one as she could only send letters, without gifts, to Australia.

She wished she was able to send something to Lolita. Had her son, Janis, had any teeth fitted, as it's not healthy to be without teeth? If needed, she could help him pay for them. Kristine also wanted to update them about what had happened to their farm. She had been unable to rescue any of their belongings as everything had been taken – even the crops had been gathered by the Langneses family. They had refused to let her in, claiming it had all been left to them. All Kristine managed to retrieve was a cupboard and a white bed, which would be sold and the money given to Zigfrids' mother. She rarely stayed in the grounds of the old farm as there were strangers who had also made their homes there. However, she had managed to retain for herself the one-roomed cottage with a small garden and apple trees. Some friends were sending their best wishes to Anna and Aiva. Also, a schoolteacher who thought Aiva had been the dearest pupil held her photo for a long time when shown it. This letter was to be passed on to Rolands to read as there was no point her writing another. She insisted that dear Rolands must write to her all about himself and his parents so that she knew everything – and who knew how long she would live! A daughter of her son Karlis, Inta, also sent her best wishes to them and had promised to write. With her sincere wishes and lots of kisses to everyone, she signed off with 'your grandmother'.

On 31 March 1958 another letter arrived for Rolands and Aiva from Kristine, now aged eighty-four years. She didn't understand why they hadn't been replying to her letters. Perhaps they had moved home and not received her letters? Or was everyone bored with writing? She wanted to know if there was a new address as she was going to send Aiva and Lolita amber necklaces. Although she had been keeping well the past year, she felt weak and there was no strength in her joints.

My great-grandmother's last letter was written on 7 January 1959. It was kept separately by my mother. She wished them all a very happy New Year and good health, and thanked them for the greetings they had sent her. She had been to visit Zigfrids' uncle (Janis Baumanis) and also his father, who wanted his son to know that he just couldn't get on with his mother, Milda, and that their marriage was not repairable. They were both at fault, so Zigfrids mustn't put all the blame on his father, she said. As for Mr Baumanis, he seemed to be a gentleman and his wife was welcoming. However, she suffered from rheumatism and the necessary medication was not available. Perhaps if they sent the prescription to Zigfrids and Aiva they could obtain it for them and put it in the post? Kristine said that she only lived for her children, but didn't feel well as she had flu and pneumonia. She was lethargic and didn't hear very well. With each passing day she felt weaker. She asked them to please write soon as she was old and ill.

Kristine died soon afterwards.

Aiva was a talented needlewoman, and made many of the garments she and Lolita wore. She also had an aggressive knitting machine, which caught her hand one time, resulting in stitches at the hospital. Both she and her mother were expert at crochet, and Anna, in particular, made beautifully intricate tablecloths and cushion covers. Lolita was probably the only one wearing home-made school summer dresses and knitted cardigans with too many buttons! Anna was a genius at creating models from papier mâché. She could literally make anything from camels to giraffes, and from monkeys to cats. She would make a wire frame and build on that, then finish with a final fabric layer. Her alligator was so well made that a toy manufacturer offered her money so that he could produce them in his factory from a mould. Surprisingly, she refused. Anna's most impressive creations were a wigwam with a Red Indian family and a large doll's house with its own walled garden and all fixtures and fittings totally handmade by her. There were shrunken heads, mini dolls, stags, lizards, and even lampshades with real dried tree leaves inset. She also had her own version of taxidermy. One that caused dogs to be upset was a stuffed fox complete with teeth, tongue and eyes, as well as four wheels so that Lolita could take it for walks. Janis even made for his little granddaughter a doll's pram comprised of metal sheets. It was so heavy that when it toppled over, Lolita could not get it upright easily.

Memories of my grandfather, Janis, are rather vague for that period in our lives. Although a bit of a character, with one glass eye and a long beard, he seemed to be just passing through life. Often he would wander off into the docklands, perhaps to a favourite pub? Perhaps he had some drinking buddies or seamen he would pass his time with? I can recall his footsteps on the deck, coming back late and singing to himself, while my grandmother was not at all pleased with him. I wonder if his life had lost all purpose as he only ever seemed to be in the background. He did enjoy his tobacco, and I can remember helping him do roll-ups with paper which he kept in a tin. He would also go fishing as it was a treat to have freshly fried fish sizzling in the pan for supper, served with tomato sauce and bread and butter. The family were also keen on the eels he caught and skinned by dropping them into boiling water, so that they literally jumped out of their skins! Needless to say, I was not keen on that delicacy! During the 1950s Janis was only in his fifties. I doubt if the combination of beer and pickled onions did his stomach any good, and his life was cut short in 1965 when he died from stomach cancer at the age of only sixty-five years.

In 1900 Zigfrids' mother, Milda Baumanis, was born on 10 January. His father, Mikels Purins, was born in 1901, on 21 May. His parents married in 1923. As a reward for being a Latvian rifleman, the country gave Mikels thirty hectares of land in the Murjanu area. Together, Milda and Mikels built their home, known as Gaujmalnieki. On 21 September 1924 twins were born to them: Zigfrids and his sister Hilda. Their christening took place in 1942 in the church in Sējas. Both were educated in Sējas Primary School. Then in Skrīveru High School they opted to specialise in agricultural studies.

Milda and Mikels lived happily together for twenty-nine years. But in 1952 Milda ended up alone after her husband left her for another woman, called Zenta. In 1956 Milda explained in a letter to her son that his father had become stupid in his old age and had left her and their home. But she had got over the heartache and all was well. Zigfrids couldn't imagine the joy Milda felt, and the happy tears she shed, when she received his letter and heard he had a wife and daughter. As she hadn't known if he was dead or alive, her hair had turned white from her worry and sadness, and she had cried every morning and every night. And now she had not just one granddaughter, but two: Anita and Lolita. She prayed to God to give them good health and success in life.

Before the Second World War, Hilda was courted by Gunars. When the Russians invaded, like many other country people they hid in the forest to avoid being sent away to Siberia. In 1949 they married and in 1950 they moved to Carnikava. Hilda gave birth to Anita in 1953. At that time Gunars was a good and loving husband. Hilda advised her brother to write to their mother in 1956, and to use her maiden name – otherwise the letter would go to their father. If Hilda ever spoke to Mikels, her husband would go crazy, which was frightening. Zigfrids also received a letter from his father's sister, Anna, in 1956. She thanked him for his letter and photo and commented that he looked different, and she said they all liked his attractive wife and daughter very much. His aunt told him that Mikels would always be his father and if he felt revengeful he might regret it one day. He knew very well that his parents hadn't got on at all, and they had both seen for themselves just how his mother had behaved towards his father. Milda had been warned she would lose her husband. And that is exactly what happened. If their children had been small, Mikels would have tolerated the atmosphere for longer. But that was how life was there: if you didn't get on, you moved on alone. Zigfrids' aunt advised him to write to his father and ask him why he had left his mother. After all, Mikels had left his home with only the clothes on his back.

In April 1956 Milda wrote again to Zigfrids. She told him that on her birthday she had cried tears of joy, knowing that her son was well. And to celebrate she had drunk a few glasses of wine. Milda looked at his photo many times a day. She went on to describe some of her interests and said she read many books and also liked to do needlework. There were also farm animals. She was only allowed one goat, which was well behaved, and she had three large sheep. One of these had three lambs, and another had two lambs. The third sheep was expecting. Milda also had two pigs, twenty chickens and two cockerels, as well as two guard dogs. She also kept beehives. Zigfrids was reminded that when he lived at home he had loved milk, honey and white bread. Milda then replied to his questions about his father, saying that he had left her for a woman of the same age. 'She' already had a daughter of thirty years of age, who had a Russian husband. 'She' had a number of Russian men, and 'that woman' lived in a house called Aizupem, not far from Murjaniem. The house didn't belong to her – it was rented. Milda no longer wanted to talk about Mikels as he was now a stranger to them as far as she was concerned. Zigfrids had asked his mother to travel to Britain to visit him and his family. She told Anna, Mikels' sister, who decided to go and see Mikels and tell him. Apparently he was really happy to hear that, as he could then sell Milda's home straight away! In future she would not be showing her letters to anyone. Mikels was not allowed anywhere near the house without her permission. At that time he'd been away for five years.

That year, Hilda also wrote to Aiva as she had been so pleased to receive a few lines from her and some photos. Hilda was very happy that her brother had a loving wife and daughter. There was a time when she would have been jealous if her brother had found a wife as she loved him very much and he meant everything to her. There is no explanation as to why Hilda would say she had to go through much because of him. But she now knew that he was happy, so she was also happy for him. Hearing that her mother, Milda, had also received a letter from Aiva, she felt ill from so much happiness! Hilda was cross with Mikels' other sister, her Aunt Alma. They had gone to visit her one Sunday in Riga, and were shocked that her father was also there with his new partner. And, to top it all, Alma had expected Hilda to be nice to her father. No, she could never be polite to him, knowing what her mother had gone through. She told Zigfrids he was never to forgive his father. And – imagine it! – 'she' wanted Mikels to sell Milda's house, just to be spiteful!

In 1959 Aiva and Zigfrids were notified that Hilda had had a major operation, which was successful, and she had made a good recovery. There were no details, but there was a comment that it was a pity Anita wouldn't gain a brother or sister.

From 11 February until 15 February 1959 I was a patient in the children's ear, nose and throat hospital in Cowbridge Road West, Ely, Cardiff. Like many children in those times, I had my tonsils and adenoids removed and can remember the jelly and ice cream we were given to help soothe our throats. I was off school until 2 March 1959.

Aiva had a few X-rays done that year. One was on 27 April 1959, when she was weighed as well, and was nine stone two and a half pounds. Another X-ray followed on 30 July 1959, when she had a slight increase in weight to nine stone four pounds. When she was weighed while having her next X-ray, on 19 November, she was nine stone six pounds. Because the results were so good, Aiva no longer needed to continue with her medication.

While Zigfrids was in and out of hospital, Rolands was planning an expedition from Cardiff to the Amazon with the MV *Tobago*. The idea was that with sufficient sponsorship the expense of the journey would be covered. As a qualified navigator and marine engineer, Zigfrids was the only one out of the male members of the family who had the essential skills to take the boat on this voyage across the ocean. However, his disabling state of health prevented him from considering making the arduous, perhaps treacherous, voyage.

Rolands planning the route of the voyage on board the Tobago.

Everyone of importance was contacted by Rolands. In January 1958 ABC Television, London, wrote a thank-you letter about the proposed journey of exploration and the possibility of a documentary film. A month later, *The Times*' advertisement department acknowledged receipt of £5 6s. for the insertion of 'Sea Voyage' in their personal column. In April there was a letter from the Reverend T. Holland at the Apostolic Delegation in London regarding the papal representative having a knowledge of missionary activities in Rio de Janeiro. He wished 'Captain' Mikelsons 'godspeed and a profitable enterprise'. In May the Venezuelan consulate in London sent information on the documents necessary for each person in the expedition. The Royal Anthropological Institute in London also considered the offer of them carrying out research.

The original plan was for the MV *Tobago* to leave Cardiff for Brazil and the Amazon, sailing via Portugal, Spain, the Canary Islands, the West Indies, Venezuela and British Guiana in July or August 1958, and to be away between twelve and eighteen months. The purpose of the voyage was to land a small team of research workers, including professional photographers, in central Brazil, where they would carry out a programme of ethnographical, zoological and botanical studies on the Rivers Tapajóz and Madeira, two of the larger tributaries of the Amazon. Special studies would be made of the little-known Indian tribes, and the flora and fauna of that region. Cine film and sound-recording apparatus would be used to make a more complete record. At the same time, the vessel would be displaying British products in the ports en route to South America. There would be advance publicity by means of television coverage, press accounts, and a special foyer display in the Capitol Cinema in Cardiff. There was a letter in July to M. D. J. Belcher, BSc, who wished to join the expedition as a botanist.

Prior to sailing, Cory Brothers & Co. Ltd would deliver to the West Dock about 3,500 gallons of diesel oil, which would be transported by their road oil tanker, which had to get alongside the vessel.

The *Tobago* had been fitted out with a large show/lounge saloon which could be converted into a small cinema to show films and lantern slides. Products could also be put on display and demonstrated.

The saloon on the Tobago.

The boat needed to be repainted, but any outside work had to be delayed due to the depressing weather. The anticipated date for setting sail was the third week in August.

Miss Eva Boehm, aged twenty-seven years, a qualified bacteriologist and microbiologist, had been recruited, and there were seven applicants for the doctor vacancy.

Eventually, the confirmed date for sailing was Wednesday 15 October 1958. The business name was accepted by the relevant authorities, and the voyage was registered as 'Expedition for Exploration and Trade'. The vessel was officially registered under its new name of MV *Tobago Explorer*.

Invitations were then sent out to attend a reception on board the *Tobago* in West Dock, Cardiff, by the captain and company of the expedition from Wales, for exploration and trade. 'Drinks and light refreshments will be served' on Wednesday 30 July 1958 at 7.30 p.m. Among those accepting were the Lord and Lady Mayoress, who were based at the Lord Mayor's Parlour in the City Hall, Cardiff.

The expedition would consist of twelve members, who included cine and still photographers, a navigator, doctors and a zoologist. Each member had to agree to contribute £150 towards the overall expenses of the trip, which had not been conceived for financial gain. However, if any profit was made, it would be divided into equal shares for each member.

The Austin Motor Company had agreed to loan a Gipsy four-wheel-drive diesel utility truck.

In addition, the medical officer owned a four-seater cabin seaplane, which would be flown down from Canada to meet them in South America.

Though the date had been fixed provisionally, the actual sailing date still depended on the completion of the necessary mechanical installation and fitting-out of the vessel, the suitability of prevailing weather conditions, and the availability of at least ten expedition members, including one experienced navigator. The decision to sail at any time would be made by the master of the *Tobago*. Even though it was anticipated that the boat would return to Great Britain within eighteen months of departure, the master did not have to guarantee return within that period.

Unfortunately, in the planning of the expedition it was found necessary to provide a considerable amount of equipment for the boat. It all had to be financed out of the expedition funds. If a bank loan turned out to be necessary, then that would be part of the funds, and would be settled on the conclusion of the expedition when back in Britain again.

The *Tobago* had attracted a lot of public attention and a group turned up in uniform from HMS *Cambria*. They were members of the Cardiff RNVR based in Sully, near Barry, the only RNR in Wales. The press accompanied them to look around the former German E-boat.

When January 1959 came, the voyage had still not taken place. If the boat could be converted into a club, a substantial sum of money would be raised and Rolands could continue with his ambitious plans for the expedition. Due to financial difficulties, the voyage just wasn't possible, even though various firms had participated and assisted in the planning. Seeing no reason as to why the boat couldn't be registered as a club, Rolands completed the necessary forms and they were forwarded to the law courts for official registration. This was followed by a visit from Inspector Knapman of the Docks Police.

The Inspector did not agree with there being a club in the docks and would not allow Rolands to continue with his plans. Rolands tried to explain that he had seen Captain Hawkins, the dock manager, who had raised no objections. However, it seems that he should have arranged a meeting with both the Dock Master and the Inspector together about the matter. As Rolands had approached this the wrong way, Inspector Knapman stubbornly would not allow him to have his boat as a club in the docks. And if he insisted on proceeding with that plan, he would be evicted from the docks. It seems the Inspector was being thoroughly awkward and unpleasant, and he complained generally about the boat. Mr Rosen, Rolands' solicitor, was asked to take the matter higher, but he finally had to admit defeat.

Mr Rosen told him, "I don't think there is anything more we can do about it."

And so the matter was dropped.

Rolands refused to give up. He wrote to Captain Hawkins asking him to come aboard as he wished to move the boat to the top end of West Dock. Permission was given for the change of location, so Rolands pushed his luck and ventured to enquire again about the club. Without hesitation, the Captain replied that it was completely out of his hands, and there was nothing at all he could do to help. He strongly advised Rolands not to carry on with the idea, and emphasised that he would never succeed.

Cousin Juris, on his travels to Jamaica and Canada, dropped in to visit his family on 9 November 1959. He wanted to spend some time with his first cousins Rolands and Aiva. It seems that Rolands still refused to totally give up on the idea of an expedition.

Rolands, after some thought, decided it might be better to try and purchase a smaller vessel and dispose of the *Tobago*. He made enquiries with James Taylor (shipbuilders) Ltd in Shoreham-by-Sea about fitting out a Halmatic hull, making it capable of commercial use between England, the West Indies and South America. They replied that they didn't make the fibreglass boats, only fitted them out. But they would pass his details on to the appropriate builder. Halmatic began constructing in 1954 the world's first GRP boat. GRP stands for glass-reinforced plastic, also known as fibreglass.

The *Perpetua* caught Rolands' eye. It was a forty-eight-foot-eight-inch motor cruiser moulded with resin. However, Rolands didn't pursue the matter; nor did he purchase another boat.

Juris with his Uncle Janis on the Tobago.

Modelling friends of Rolands on the deck of the Tobago.

As a result of all the publicity about the voyage to the Amazon, the boat attracted a lot of attention and celebrities. Joan Collins at the time was under contract to Twentieth Century Fox, but came to London to visit her parents. She decided to visit the *Tobago* while in Britain, and Rolands succeeded in persuading her to model for him. The most famous British blonde bombshell of the 1950s was Diana Dors – a popular actress from Swindon – and Rolands must have very happily given her a tour of the boat.

In 1958 Shirley Bassey released her first single, 'Kiss Me, Honey Honey, Kiss Me'. She had yet to hit fame and fortune when she wore a luxurious white fur coat on the same bus I was travelling in when I visited the boat in Tiger Bay. Although young, I loved the song and knew who she was!

While Rolands and his parents were still living on the *Tobago*, Cliff Richard performed in Cardiff in 1960 and decided to drop in on them. Anna always remembered him as being that 'nice boy'. Lolita regretted not having been there that day.

In November 1961 the MV *Tobago* was sadly sold as the maintenance became too costly. She became a floating nightclub off the coast of France, while in the ownership of a Greek magnate.

The ambitious hopes and aspirations to explore the amazing Amazon became just a voyage of dreams.

Zigfrids and Aiva had decided to give up their involvement in the voyage. Ziggy had regular employment with City Motors Ltd and was able to fulfil their dream of buying a house at last. In June 1960 they moved from Kingsland Road and paid a weekly amount to the original owner of their new home until the total amount had been paid. In those days there was no way of obtaining a mortgage from the bank.

Before moving away, Janis decided to try and catch one of the feral kittens in the dock railway sheds. She was a feisty little creature and sank her needle-like sharp teeth into his hand. She had to be caged until she eventually calmed down. And thus her name was Minnie the Minx. Minnie became an affectionate member of the family and tolerated my dressing her up and putting her in my doll's pram. However, being feral remained in her blood. She would like to wander off, sometimes for days. In the kitchen was a big black fireplace and she disappeared up the chimney. When retrieved, her white bib and four white socks were black like the rest of her, so we had to block the chimney up with newspaper unless it was being used.

Rolands had nowhere to live once the boat was sold, so he was offered a room in Aiva and Ziggy's house. He lived in their large front bedroom until March 1965, and until the money from the boat sale had been frittered away. As Rolands needed income, he decided to concentrate on being a graphic designer and artist. He continued to wish that one day he would be the owner of another boat. The *Tobago*'s sale gave him the time and money to entertain lady friends. A young lady called Shirley, with short, dark curly hair, was in his life for a couple of years. When Lolita passed her eleven-plus exam in 1963, Shirley gave her a boxed book: *Jane Eyre*, by Charlotte Brontë. Rolands was generous with money and would often take Lolita to the cinema, and treat her to a weekly lunch. She was also allowed to buy any 45-rpm pop record that she chose. Some lunches were at the large Cardiff department stores, where catwalk models would parade between the tables, displaying the latest fashions on offer in the clothes department. Rolands had the foreign charm that tempted the models to join them at the table. They were always friendly to the young girl with him and one model took off the silver bracelet she wore to give it to Lolita, who was admiring it.

By 1968 Rolands had established a design and card-printing business in Kings Road, Canton, Cardiff.

An example of graphic design by Rolands.

A Welsh design by Rolands – signed 'R. M.' at the bottom edge.

Sometimes Rolands would pop into his local church, St Catherine's Anglican Church, although he was Lutheran and used to go to the Norwegian church in the docks. Dorothy had started attending St Catherine's in 1966/67. And it was there that Rolands first saw her. She was a Girl Guide leader, and her original company was attached to Cathedral Road Presbyterian Church in Pontcanna, which was around the corner from her home in Conway Road. Rolands was often seen at St Catherine's events with Dorothy, but he wasn't a regular at the Sunday morning service. She is remembered fondly by many of the parishioners as she did so much for the church, including organising coffee mornings and arranging fundraising events. However, Dorothy's family believe that Rolands first saw her on the day Philip and Kate were married. Philip worked with Rolands and invited him to the ceremony. Dorothy and her sisters, Cynthia and Brenda, were also at the wedding in March 1968, which was held at St Isan Church in Llanishen. They had hoped Rolands would aim his attentions at Cynthia, as she was available, pretty and enjoyed male company. But for some reason unknown to them he targeted Dorothy, who seemed a very unlikely match for love. She had never been one to have time for romance and was generally not keen on the male species. She didn't attract male attention, although her looks were pleasant enough. But Dorothy was very hospitable, a good cook, ambitious and loved her mother dearly. Rolands obviously decided she would make him a good wife and saw further than just her looks.

Dorothy Elizabeth Williamson was born on 15 February 1929 in Newport, South Wales. Her father's work took him to London, where they lived until war broke out. Dorothy was in a cinema near her home when the Crystal Palace was destroyed by one of the greatest fires ever seen in London, on 30 November 1936. They rescued a cat from the fire and he was given the apt name of Sooty. Because of the war breaking out, Dorothy, like many other children, was sent away to the safety of the Welsh countryside and spent her early years on a farm with horses in Llanelli. The family then lived for a short time in Cardiff, where they rented a house in Dryburgh Avenue, and Dorothy was a pupil at Birchgrove School. When war ended, she started working for Sun Life of Canada, in their various offices, until she retired. She was considered a valuable member of their staff and received a generous pension from them. Dorothy's parents divorced when her father met someone else – someone he fell in love with, and remained with for the rest of his life. Dorothy settled at 68 Conway Road, Penhill, Cardiff, with her mother. However, she found it difficult going to Girl Guide camps, on hikes with the girls, or for trips away as she felt she couldn't leave her mother. She admitted to Sue Parsons, who was one of her flock, that she had a friend, Rolands, whom she cared for very much. But it was a difficult situation: her mother didn't know about him as Dorothy didn't think her mother would approve. Nobody – not even close friends – had any idea that Rolands was still legally married to Rasma. In the meantime, Dorothy was gently courted by Rolands, who patiently bided his time.

At the age of ten, in the winter of early 1963, when we had heavy snowfall, I was really poorly. My mother diagnosed mumps. My neck was swollen and I was unable to attend my regular ballroom dance classes. From 1962 to 1964 I belonged to Victor Sylvester Junior Club and received birthday greeting telegrams from them. I couldn't attend Sunday school, let alone go to the junior school when the new term started at Marlborough Road, on 10 January. I suffered for two weeks at home before the doctor examined me and decided I needed emergency treatment. The ambulance came for me and I underwent an operation for an abscess. If it had burst, my life would have been threatened. The operation was at 11 p.m. on 14 January and my parents visited the following evening. I can remember that my wound was packed with dressing, which was removed when the weeping ceased. Unfortunately, I was left with a permanent scar on my neck. Snow covered the ground until the end of February. I missed my mock eleven-plus exam as I had to stay in hospital until 26 January. When I returned home, I still felt unwell for a few days. I had studied while in hospital and the school had supplied me with the appropriate exercise books to help me pass my tests in English, maths, music, science and Welsh. Even though my parents were not fluent in English, or familiar with the teaching methods, I was a good student with their help. I was allowed to sit my missed exam.

On 16 June 1963 I sat my dance exam in the waltz. The Imperial Society of Teachers of Dancing examined us at the Victor Sylvester Junior Club in the ballroom downstairs in the Capitol Cinema. The remarks were that my dancing was, 'careful', and I was awarded the Junior Bronze Medal, as I was 'commended'. The 13th of October 1963 was the date of my next ballroom dance exam. I was 'commended' again with even higher marks, but was still awarded the Junior Bronze Medal in the quickstep. I was only four marks short of the eighty-five needed to gain an 'honours'. At the same session I was also 'commended' again in the foxtrot. The remark by the examiner was 'very good use of feet', and I was awarded yet another Junior Bronze Medal. A year later I was still ballroom dancing.

I used to go to Sunday school at the local Methodist church on the corner of Wellfield Road and Albany Road in Roath, with my best friend, Christine Lloyd. We became friends after I moved to Kimberley Road, as she lived only a street away, at 28 Mafeking

Road. We both passed our eleven-plus exam, and we were so happy to be selected to attend the same secondary school. We were pupils at Lady Margaret High School for Girls, in Colchester Avenue. However, we went through school in different classes and had our own group of friends. But we remained good friends throughout our lives. I enjoyed my first year at my new school as we had 'record hops' and learned dances such as the shake and the twist. Cookery lessons involved creating dishes such as apple fruit sponge, syrup flapjacks, jam tarts, salmon fishcakes, Scotch eggs, shortbread and fairy cakes. One time, my grandfather came to the school to walk me home, and helped carry my dish full of casserole. Unfortunately, the lid was loose, and he ended up wearing some of the contents!

In those days we had swimming lessons. The Guildford Crescent or Corporation Baths were built in 1862, and from 1958 became used exclusively by children. I was never an able swimmer and only managed to complete forty-five widths out of the sixty required to get a certificate. I did manage to dive off the side of the pool, but almost drowned when I found myself out of my depth, as I panicked. The baths closed in 1984 and were demolished. I was never sporty, but we were lucky to have a lot of ground surrounding the school and could play hockey in all weathers, wearing just our PE outfits. I did enjoy playing rounders and tennis, and was awarded 'high standard' for the long jump. I think most of us hated the communal showers, but we were trim and fit from all the exercise.

A highlight in 1964 was my meeting Roger Moore on 9 May. At that time he was 'The Saint' (TV series), and made an appearance at the Welsh Ideal Home Exhibition in Sophia Gardens. Roger was hugely popular, and I was very lucky to personally get his autograph in my red autograph book, which I still have. His smashing smile was one to remember too.

In April my grandparents went to live in Kidwelly, in a caravan with chickens. Then in the September the doctor diagnosed Janis as having an ulcer in the bottleneck of his stomach. He came to live with us while Anna moved their belongings into their new flat.

That year I was also fitted with braces on my teeth. My front teeth were crooked due to overcrowding in my mouth, and that resulted in having some teeth removed to make space for movement.

School outings included trips to Porthkerry Park, Caerphilly Castle, St Fagans and Castell Coch. My lessons generally went well and I received commendations in chemistry, graphs, geography, scripture, history, music, algebra, art and English.

I had a good friend called Dzintra Vizbulis, daughter of close Latvian friends of my parents. They lived in Swansea, firstly in Rosehill Terrace, then at 12 Llewelyn Circle. Our fathers were ardent fishermen, and in June we went midnight fishing during the full moon. We walked a long way along the Gower beach until we reached the sea. Our shoes and socks were soaked through, so we decided we might as well paddle in them. We saw plenty of jellyfish on the sand and had to be careful not to step on them. Our fathers waded out into the water with a large net. This they repeated five times until they'd caught plenty of fish. The moon cast a silvery glow over the sea. At 4 a.m. we were back at Dzintra's home, frozen through. The following month Dzintra and her parents came to visit. Her father, Imants, had caught a three-foot-four-inch pike, weighing seventeen pounds, which was to be our meal the next day. In August I spent a week in Swansea with Dzintra and we had a fun-filled time going to the beach, shopping, flirting with the lads at the funfair and playing minigolf. We saw the Beatles' new film, *Hard Day's Night*, at the Plaza, which was packed with screaming fans. Dzintra then came to stay a week with us.

In October my parents decided they would like to move to a smaller, more manageable house – one that didn't have rising damp and didn't need new windows. We also had lodgers to help pay the bills. They started house-hunting and had seen a couple they thought might be suitable. A month later, some viewers showed interest in purchasing our home, so my parents had another look at a house they liked. 30 Kimberley Road was bought by Kenneth Bristow for him and his son and daughter, Nadwyn and Jean. There was also a little boy called Philip. They had been lodgers with us at one time. When Kenneth died in

1979, the house was sold for £29,000. It was now worth almost double. At last, Sunday 17 January 1965 was removal day to 17 Queensberry Road in the Cyncoed area. It was a modern former show house, with a separate garage. My parents had the front bedroom; I had the back bedroom overlooking the woods. And there was only a small box room, so there was no longer space for any lodgers. Rolands had to move in with Anna and Janis, who had moved into their new home at 17 Ninian Road, in the Roath Park area. My uncle never seemed to have any money to spend on his lady friends. He was an artist, but unable to earn enough money to manage. I was with my mother when she was very upset at discovering her brother had stolen over £10 – her saved holiday money, kept in the bottom of her wardrobe. Rolands did confess and promised to repay the missing amount. I think Mother was relieved at not having him live with us, especially as he often didn't get up until lunchtime. We had our first ever telephone fitted, with a shared line, and when it rang for the first time it was a wrong number! My uncle and grandparents didn't stay long in their house and moved again, this time to their new flat in Ty-Gwyn Road, Penylan.

According to my diary, my ambition in life was to be someone like Cathy McGowan in the TV series *Ready Steady Go*, or be a fan-club secretary, or perhaps even a doctor, as I was fascinated by human biology.

On 3 March we had the worst blizzard in Wales for twenty years. We visited my grandfather on 5 March, as he was feeling poorly and was in great pain. We saw him again the following day as we were worried about him.

At school we started having needlework lessons instead of cookery, and our first attempt was to make a petticoat with our own drawn pattern.

My grandfather grew worse and, unfortunately, on 26 March he had to go into hospital, and we visited him in Llandough Hospital. He was then moved to Penarth Hospital as he was not suffering from an ulcer, but had stomach cancer. We visited him there and were advised not to tell him he was dying, as he thought he was getting better. The pain-relieving injections of morphine made him more cheerful. We visited again on the 16th, then my parents visited him without me on the 18th as he was very much worse. On Easter Monday, the 19th, Janis died. He was only sixty-five years of age.

On 22 April we went to see my grandfather laid to rest in the funeral chapel. He was clad in silks and frills in the coffin. Rolands did not pay his respects as he wanted his last memories of his father to be happy ones. The funeral was on 26 April 1965, at 11 a.m. There were lots of flowers, and my father took photos of the burial. His passing away was the first big loss in my life. I was very fond of my 'Opap', as I would call him.

Before the end of term, our school trip was to Cheddar. We crossed the Bristol Channel from Cardiff Docks by steamer, and landed in Weston-super-Mare, where we had lunch on the beach. I had four rides on the donkeys and two on the ponies, costing 6d. a ride. We were then taken to Cheddar Caves by coach, which took an hour. The caves were beautiful and the gorges were tremendously high and breathtaking. We had some tea before heading back home. At 7.35 p.m. we arrived back at Cardiff Docks, where my father met me and Christine, and took her home to Mafeking Road, where she still lived.

Across the road from us lived a young student doctor with his sister, Angela, and their parents. I took a fancy to Michael Rowe as he would always say hello to me and give me a wink. Top Rank was immensely popular and had morning disco sessions for youngsters on a Saturday. I managed to persuade Michael to give me a lift into town, where I met my school friend Sandra at Top Rank. Michael liked to pop in and see my parents, often staying for a few hours. I think they became a little concerned as they asked Mike if he'd like me as a sister. I remember him showing me the Pygmy skeleton in his bedroom.

In October I graduated to Saturday afternoon sessions at Top Rank. One day I had seven dances with boys – six with the same one! He introduced himself as Don. He liked my long hair and said it was beautiful. We smooched (popular on the dance floor in those days). He took my telephone number and kissed me goodbye.

My parents were very sociable in those days. Christmas morning involved having drinks at the home of Mr and Mrs Monks in the next road. Then in the evening we had all the Rowe family over for drinks. Around 12.30 a.m. we played records and danced. Mike couldn't do the waltz, but we did quite nicely just stepping about. But he could dance fabulously to disco music. He would hold me close when slow dancing, squeeze my hand and grip my waist. On leaving at 5 a.m., he kept his arm around my waist for a while. As far as I was concerned, it was my best Christmas ever. Early on New Year's Day, around 12.30 a.m. people came flocking to our house as we were having a party. I hardly knew half of them. There must have been about twenty guests, all dancing until the bitter end at 4 a.m.

We were now in 1966, and the highlight of that year was probably my going to see the Walker Brothers perform at the Capitol on Friday 15 April. Also starring were Roy Orbison and Lulu. The queue in had extended a long way down Churchill Way. I bought a large poster of Scott Walker, eighteen inches by twenty-three inches, for two shillings and sixpence. The show started on time. I was seated in the dress circle, Block B, Seat C38, so I had an excellent view of my heart-throb Scott Walker. He wore a pair of grey jeans with a shiny silver zip. He bent down and shook his head of wavy locks, and the girls really screamed. Gary got up from his drums and also sang, dancing a bit. John looked fabulous with his long hair slightly wavy at the sides. Their performance was excellent. Next to appear was Lulu minus the Luvvers. She looked pretty in a blue suit and her hair in a mod style. The last to come on stage was Roy Orbison. Personally, I was not a fan, but he was a good singer. It was all over by 8.15 p.m. and I stumbled out, all dreamy-eyed after seeing Scott in such a fantastic show.

Saturday 25 June was the first time we travelled abroad for our holiday, touring the continent. I was very excited and looked forward to my two-week vacation. We left home at 9.40 a.m. with all our camping gear piled on the car. We arrived in Dover at 9.30 p.m. and had a look at the White Cliffs, which are not all that white, but very picturesque. After supper in a restaurant, we walked around until it was time to board the ferry at 11 p.m. The *Koningin Fabiola* left port at 11.45 p.m. and we arrived in Ostend at 4 a.m., having managed to snooze a little on board. Fifteen minutes later we drove out of the port and Father remembered to drive on the right-hand side of the road. It was pouring with rain. We drove through Jabbeke, Brugge, Oostkamp, Beernem and Aalter. Around 5.15 p.m. we stopped for a while and had a rest. At 2 p.m. we reached Luxembourg and at 2.45 p.m. we arrived at the German border, where we changed our Belgian money into pfennigs and marks. At 5.30 p.m. we stopped in Zweibrücken, where we set camp in the pouring rain and had to rescue our belongings from the puddles in the tent. In the evening we took a walk, passing the rose gardens, then crossing a bridge in a park where there was also a waterfall. We then came across a dance hall where we could hear a group playing, and saw young Germans going in and out. Then it was back to camp and to our beds. The next morning we awoke at 7.15 a.m. to the sound of building work and trains. Very noisy. We packed up after breakfast and left at 10 a.m. in the rain again. At 5.55 p.m. we arrived at Rottweil, then we headed for Meersburg, where we set up camp by Lake Bodensee, also known as Lake Constance.

Our striped car parked next to Mr and Mrs Monks' white car.

On Tuesday when we awoke we could hear the wind roaring and our tent was flapping like crazy. It was also freezing cold. The tree we were underneath was full of cherries and our tent was covered with squashed fruit. Father climbed up the tree and passed down the delicious cherries for us to eat. The lake was really beautiful. It became warmer later, but then we had more rain again. I wrote some postcards. We were doing the tour with our neighbours, Mr and Mrs Monks, but we were only meeting up at prearranged points. This was one place where we joined up for a drink then went for a walk down to the lakeside, through some woods. We then had supper and retired for the night.

The next morning we got up early as we had to pack up all our camping gear. At 11.45 a.m. we reached the Austrian border and changed our money into schillings. Beautiful mountain scenery, but it was very cold and we had snow all around us. We descended from the mountains, leaving the snow behind. At 5.20 p.m. we were well on our way to the Italian border. We didn't see any sunshine until 6.30 p.m. We were refused entry into Italy as we didn't have the necessary documents. So we had a quick look around Alassio, then turned the car around and found a place to camp in Pfunds. After supper we went for a walk and saw old, unusual houses. There were also jolly young men singing and yodelling.

On Thursday the 30th we rose at 7.45 a.m. and packed up after breakfast. We were surrounded by the Tyrolean mountains. Late morning we arrived in Innsbruck, pitched our tent, had lunch, then walked into town, which turned out to be some distance away. We shopped for souvenirs, ate frankfurters and bread from a food stall, then arrived back at camp at 8.30 p.m. feeling rather weary. Friday turned out to be a lovely warm day, around 85°F. We had a leisurely day. In the evening we went to a Tyrolean show held in the town centre. The yodelling and dancing didn't finish until 11 p.m.

On Saturday 2 July we rose early, packed bread rolls, butter and other foodstuffs and drove to Zugspitze, the highest mountain in Germany. We ascended by cable car and saw spectacular scenery. The ride to the top took twelve minutes as it is 2,963 metres high.

It was cold and snow-covered and only 5°C. Next we headed for Königschloss Castle. It was a very long and steep walk up to the castle, which was breathtaking. We were back in Innsbruck at 10.30 p.m. after a tiring but interesting day.

Sunday was very hot and I wore a swimsuit for the first time this holiday. Later on we went to the Alpine Zoo, which was closed, so we aimed for the Royal Gardens, which are beautifully floodlit on summer evenings. There was an open-air stage on which a group played, and teenagers danced on the small dance floor in front of the stage.

On Monday the 4th we packed up and drove to Salzburg. We visited Berchtesgaden to see the Eagle's Nest, which was Hitler's hideout during the war. We had to take a coach ride up because of the narrow roads and hairpin bends. When we reached the large platform, we took the lift up to the Eagle's Nest. The stunning shiny brass lift was specially built for Hitler. We didn't have too much time to linger over the lovely views. We arrived back in Salzburg in the evening and located our campsite next door to a school. We unpacked again, then had supper and went for a walk by the River Salzack. The beautiful fountain, adorned with figures of horses, was shown in the film *The Sound of Music*. We also saw Salzburg Castle. We had an enjoyable evening, relaxing and drinking beer in a beer garden. Then it was back to camp and to bed. In the middle of the night the sound of thunder woke me up.

The 5th was a hot, uncomfortable day at 87°F. In the town we had a cool drink and some cakes in an open-air café, in the shade of the trees. Back at camp, it began to rain. When I was in the shower there was a loud clap of thunder so loud it made the building shake! In the evening we went to the Café Winkler, which was sited up a mountain, with a lift up to it. A group played and at 10 p.m. the dance began. Later on an elderly gentleman invited me, in German, to dance with him. I had to tell him in my best schoolgirl German that I didn't speak the language. We stayed until the band stopped playing, then walked back to the camp in the rain.

After lunch the next day, we went into town to do some

shopping. I bought more postcards. I also wanted a red Austrian hat for me, which I managed to buy in a shop that specialised in national costume and accessories. In a souvenir shop I bought a fluffy white feather and two souvenir brooches to decorate my new hat. I also bought a pretty souvenir bookmark, which I still have. We looked around the Mirabell Gardens, which were very pretty. There were statues by the entrance, a fountain in the middle and a rose garden at the end. At the side of the gardens was a long overgrown archway, through which we strolled. There was also another fountain in the centre with a horse that had wings. Salzburg is Mozart's birthplace so we bought Mozart cakes as souvenirs. In the evening it began to rain again, but this time it poured all night. My parents had to dig holes to try and create some drainage. There were puddles inside and around the tent. They ended up having to pack away most of the contents and the bedding to stop everything becoming wet. I slept with my clothes on as it was so cold and by then I didn't have all my bedding. A very uncomfortable night!

Lolita admiring the gardens.

It was now Thursday the 7th and it rained again later in the morning. Our airbeds were slightly damp as some of last night's rain had seeped into the separate bedroom. After breakfast we packed up and left at 11.45 a.m., heading for München (Munich). We drove past many vineyards with vines twice the height of a man. We arrived there at 1.30 p.m., and then decided to drive to Frankfurt, where we arrived at 7.45 p.m. It was still raining, so we carried on to Köln (Cologne) and arrived there at 10.15 p.m. We found a campsite and put up our tent.

Next morning we awoke around 10 a.m. As mother had a headache, we delayed going into the town centre until late afternoon. To reach the town we had to use the car as we needed to cross the River Rhine and park on the other side. We decided to look around the old cathedral. Parts of it had been damaged during the Second World War. It was really breathtaking. It was tall and there were hundreds of life-size and small figures decorating it. We couldn't go in as it was now too late, but we heard how disappointing the interior was, as the original stained-glass windows had been replaced by plain windows when the glass had been shattered in the war. Later on I had some chips, which were called *frittes*, and were eaten with a small plastic fork out of a cone-shaped paper bag. We returned to camp late, had supper and went to bed.

Our final day was Saturday 9 July, when we got up early and packed up everything. We stopped at the campsite shop at the entrance to the site. Mother wanted to buy a few last-minute souvenirs, and she came out with a large china vase, a cute toy lion and a set of glasses decorated with vintage cars. We left at 11.30 a.m. There were some smart stores in the town centre, including a Woolworth and a C&A. By 1 p.m. we were back in Belgium, where it began to rain. My father put his foot down on the accelerator and we reached the fantastic speed of 150 km/h, which is around 80 mph, and arrived in Ostend at 5.40 p.m. After eating some delicious chips, we decided to see if we could board the ferry that night instead of the next day, as booked. So at 6.55 p.m. we boarded the *Roi Baudouin*, and sailed from port at 7.15 p.m. We remained on the deck most of the time, enjoying the crossing. At 11.35 p.m. we drove into Dover, having driven 2,061 miles in our Singer Gazelle.

After stopping only once for some sleep, we arrived home at 8.30 a.m., having had a smashing holiday and wishing to do it all again, though only if we had a longer time to enjoy it at a more leisurely pace – and less rain, of course.

My school report was waiting for me. I was very pleased to be second in my class, and that my next form would be 4B.

'Uncle' Juris dropped in to see us for a few days on 26 July, and promised to visit again the following year.

Mike was still a focus of my attention. On 22 August it was his birthday, so I went across the road with my father to see him and give him a box of Black Magic chocolates. I received a thank-you kiss. To celebrate I had my arm twisted to drink a vodka and lemonade followed by a vodka and lime. Every time I looked at Mike he would wink at me. We left at 12.45 a.m. I have to admit I enjoyed his attention as I was a flirtatious young lady.

In October there was a careers convention at school, and it was suggested I could be an architect, an engineer or even a German physicist!

We had new neighbours at number 15 – John and Pamela Dodd, who invited us to their house-warming party. Mother was having her hair done at home, so Father and I went without her; then she joined us at 10.30 p.m. I enjoyed a vodka and lime, then a sherry. It became very crowded, so we went to John's parents' home in Colchester Avenue as it was much larger and more spacious, like Buckingham Palace! I really didn't want any more to drink, but Pamela insisted I had more sherry. We really enjoyed ourselves, but had to make our excuses at 1 a.m. as I had school the next morning suffering from a sore head.

When school broke up for half-term on 21 October, I had the great news that I had won a school prize.

The Howardian School for Boys was next door to my school, and they held their Christmas dance on 25 November. I persuaded Mike to take me. A group called The Fabs was performing. We had a lovely time, close dancing and holding hands. I wore my very long hair in a side plait and wore a blue smock, and I was told how nice I looked. I really liked Mike. We left at 11 p.m., having had an unforgettable evening.

Christmas 1966 turned out to be another very sociable one. Mr and Mrs Monks popped in for a drink, then we went over to their house. We had more drinks at Christine's house, then went back home, where Rolands and his mother joined us for our festive turkey dinner. Later on, the Rowe family came over. Rolands danced with Angela, and I danced with Mike. We slow-danced through all the records, whatever the tempo. Father put a stop to the records, but the party continued until 5 a.m. with a lot of laughs and hugs all round.

Next day, our neighbours Pam and John came in for a drink and ended up staying until 2 a.m.

On the 27th we decided to go visiting and saw the Spalvainis family. The Upmācis family were also there, having come all the way from London.

The year ended with drinks at Pam and John's, visiting Granny Anna (my 'Omam'), then a New Year toast with the Rowes. As you can guess, my favourite male for 1966 had been Michael Rowe.

During 1967 I continued to flirt with various young men, but I was also busy sitting exams, with generally good results. Mike was still in and out of my life, but by March I had decided that perhaps my crush on him had waned. Considering how young I was, perhaps that was sensible of me.

In February our school became involved with the Electrical Association for Women, which was based at 25 Foubert's Place, London, W1. The EAW taught us young ladies 'practical and theoretical knowledge of the use and care of Domestic Electrical Equipment'. I did exceedingly well and was awarded the Home Electricity Certificate, having passed with 'distinction'.

That month I also bought a terrapin in a pet shop. It was a new fad then and no one really knew how to care for them properly. Poor Kinky ended up not living a long and healthy life.

In March our headmistress, Miss Curtis, announced the names of those who had gained honours in their subjects, and our positions in class. Amazingly, I achieved honours in maths and art.

On 20 April the school arranged for every pupil in the school to be in just one photo. This was achieved by the professional photographer taking a panoramic shot. The problem was that this photo was so large that I decided to cut it into three so that it could be displayed in my album.

A special event for me was on 26 April 1967, when the Walker Brothers came to Cardiff again and appeared at the Capitol Cinema at 6.15 p.m. My mother came with me this time and we arrived at the venue at 6.05 p.m. We were well positioned in our twelve-shillings-and-sixpence seats. The tension was great before the show started. When the lights went down, the screaming was ear-piercing. First to be introduced were The Quotations, who were quite good. Next to appear were The Californians, who went down well with the crowd as they looked great and sounded good. Then there was Engelbert Humperdinck, who did a really surprising routine. Usually he looked quiet and decent on television, but onstage he twisted, kicked his legs and behaved in a sexy manner! Mother really enjoyed herself as Engelbert was her favourite singer. During the interval I looked through the programme, which had fantastic pictures of the Walker Brothers on the cover and inside. The Quotations opened the second half. Then there was Cat Stephens, for whom nearly everyone stood on their seats and frantically waved their hands and other items. I couldn't restrain myself any longer and stood up as well. I grabbed the scarf from around Mother's neck and waved it while bobbing up and down on my seat. And finally the Walker Brothers appeared. I was so excited I nearly fell off my seat! Scott was fantastic. In fact they all were. Mother had to give in and stood up as well since she could no longer see anything. She commented that I was creating a breeze with her scarf! Their performance did not last long enough. They sang many songs and I was worn out by the time the curtains closed. This had been their last tour. Mother had also enjoyed herself. I bought pictures of Cat, Scott and the Walker Brothers, and Mother actually treated herself by buying one of Engelbert. Father picked us up and we arrived home feeling very happy.

On 6 May 1967 I had managed to sign up seventeen sponsors for a charity walk. The Cardiff Society for Mentally Handicapped

Children was raising funds to build their own swimming pool. 'Tramp 23' was to take place at 1 p.m. and the walk would be twenty-three miles through the surrounding countryside and across Caerphilly Mountain. It would start at the Melbourne Motor Company car park in Cardiff and finish in Harriet Street, Cardiff. In the morning it rained, but it cleared up later. I wore ankle-length nylons, green slacks, my mother's red-and-black cotton jumper, my yellow cardigan and an anorak. Mike Rowe gave me a lift to the start, where I handed in my sponsor list and was given ticket number 20. I waited for Juliette, Angela, Valmai, Chloe and Anne to turn up, then we set off at 1.15 p.m. It drizzled for a while. The walk up Caerphilly Mountain was tiring. We trudged mile after mile. Poor Juliette gave up after fourteen miles. There were free biscuits and milk for refreshment. I had my own orange squash and a sandwich. I changed my shoes for more-comfortable slippers, and ate some apple. And I dumped my bag in a marshal's car. They were also picking up weary walkers. My feet were now killing me, but I carried on. It rained a few more times. I was taken by surprise when we walked up Llanedeyrn Road, as it led past my house, then also passed Granny's flat. Finally we reached the end of the twenty-three miles and collapsed on some chairs. Valmai's father, Mr James, was kind enough to take me home, where I arrived at 8.30 p.m., hardly able to walk any further. I soaked my feet and put lots of talcum powder on them. I also found two or three painful blisters. My total sponsorship money added up to £9 4s. By Monday, although my muscles still ached, I was able to play tennis at school, unlike the others who had done the walk.

Father often drove us to Barry Island in the evenings, when we were peckish, so that we could indulge in a takeaway meal. We would eat in the car, steaming up the windows. We loved beefburgers, which cost us one shilling and sixpence each. Around 11 p.m. we would be sitting in the car, relishing them.

That year we also had a beautiful dog, which I was always taking for walks. She was a red Irish setter and also an escape artist! Strangers were always bringing her home. On 3 August 1967 Sunits (Latvian for doggy) vanished again, through the back garden fence. Father waited until the following day to see if she was in kennels, or whether the police had found her. He was told that she was in a house on King George V Drive, as an elderly couple there had found her. If no one had claimed Sunits, they would have kept her. Father returned home with her and we were happy to have her back. But she was hungry, she could hardly walk, and was so tired she fell asleep on the kitchen floor. However, that experience didn't stop her roaming – four days later she had gone again. When she was returned on the 10th, she looked even better than before she went! After a bath, she was lovely and clean and probably pondering about her next expedition.

Our beautiful red setter.

When we lived in Kimberley Road, my father used to do private car mechanical work in our garage at the bottom of the garden. Access was via the lane. He worked well into the night and had many customers who trusted him to do a good reliable job on their vehicles. When we moved to Queensberry Road he had enough customers to open up his own business, and Z. P. Motors Ltd was born at 42 Elm Street Lane, situated off City Road.

My father's pickup truck.

August 1967 was an eventful summer for me. On Saturday the 19th I went off to Latvian 'summer camp', which was held in Almeley, near Hereford, in a large country house with grounds and a lake. We left home at 11 a.m. and arrived there at 2.30 p.m. Among the youngsters I found a new friend, Mara Zolnerciks, also fifteen years old. She was from Tuffley in Gloucester. We all spent the day just settling in and getting to know each other. Sunday was leisurely as there was nothing to do even though the sun shone brightly. It worried me a little when our leader, Mr Kazocins, said that if we thought we were there to play and not work, then we could go home tomorrow. In the evening we all went to the pub, but Mara and I returned to camp earlier than everyone else as we were feeling a little bored. The next evening at the pub was more fun.

On Tuesday 22 August we were up at 7.30 a.m. After breakfast there were two discussions on art. Then we were free until lunch. As it was so hot I went paddling in my shorts and shirt blouse. Some of the boys commented on my long loose hair. Lunch was served at 1 p.m. and was followed by more free time until our afternoon tea at 4 p.m., and again until dinner at 7 p.m. We sat through a slideshow on art, but found it unbearably hot in the room. Then we were off to the pub, the Bell Inn, again. Mara, Maya and I had a refreshing cider. I wore my black dress, my small earrings, my heart necklace, and my hair loose. Dace Lusis, from Keighley, had a gin and orange. Paul and John were also there. Later on, Indra Vilks, from Bushbury, came in with Anna Balodis, from Leeds, then Ruta and some others. Unfortunately, the landlord decided to insist that everyone under eighteen years of age had to get out. We stayed put until the landlord telephoned the big house. At that point we hurriedly exited! I took a liking to both Paul and Valdis.

Wednesday 23 August was another nice day. I wore my yellow trousers, my V-necked white jumper with long sleeves, and my hair loose again. As I was in group 3, we had our photos taken after lunch. The bus came at 2.30 p.m. and we set off for the Black Mountains in Wales. When the bus parked in Hay, we were given a bag of sandwiches and a bottle of squash to share between five of us. It was uphill all the way from there. Mara, Andra Ozols from Wednesfield, Daina Grigjanis from Leeds, Charlie, Andris, Janis and I slowly moved ahead and we lost sight of all the others. At 4 p.m. it was time to head back. We messed around, throwing water at each other. It then began to rain and I was worried my camera and transistor radio would get wet. Mara, Daina and I were lagging behind, so we thought it would be funny to thumb a lift. When a Mini stopped with two ladies inside, they surprised us with an offer of a lift back to Hay. We accepted and passed the others, who were envious when they saw us. Two female teachers tried to protect themselves from the rain with their cardigans. Mr Kazocins and our group leader were already waiting for our bus to arrive. We were relieved to get back to base. In the evening, after dinner, there were no discussions. Instead we were outdoors watching the rowing competition. Valdis Bergmans came first by rowing four times across the lake in fifty minutes. Then there was a tug of war. We asked permission and were allowed to go to The Pheasant. I wore my red skirt and tied my hair back with a nylon scarf. When we returned to the house, Rita, Dace, Juris and I went on the lake, with lovely Valdis rowing the boat. As it was so dark we were forbidden to go near the water at night. When there was lightning we became quite scared. Back ashore, Valdis gave me a helping hand out of the boat. I felt sure he must be older than the thirteen years he claimed, as he was so tall, dark, handsome and masculine.

On Friday morning we had the last of our discussions. Mr Celms took part when we were talking about the list we had made of what we considered the most important things in our lives. Everyone had put love first and church near the bottom. Before dinner I changed into my chiffon dress and put a scarf in my plait. Mr Kazocins made a closing speech while everyone was gathered around the flagpole. After dinner, prizes were distributed by Andris to the winners of the various sports events. Valdis won a watermelon for his rowing, and his navigator won a lemon. A young man wearing braces, and a flower in his hat, won a tin of Kennomeat for being the worst player in the volleyball team. And so it went on. Then we were off to the pub for the last time. I had half a pint of cider and a gin and orange, as well as a sip of lager and lime. I felt a little tipsy and was rather merry on the way back. We thumbed a lift and were picked up by Richard and Mr Kazocins' son. I changed my outfit again and put on my yellow trousers with a white skinny-rib top. We went down to the bonfire and I persuaded Mara to cook me a sausage as I wasn't too steady on my feet.

When Valdis saw me in the dark he asked, "Who is that?"
To this I replied, "Me!"
He came over and put his arm around me. His mother made a surprise appearance and told him off. She took him away, but he managed to return after a while. He put his arm around me

and asked if I'd like to go for a walk. I agreed, but he'd had too much to drink and couldn't walk straight. Then he had to lie down on the grass a couple of times. We looked at the stars, which was kind of romantic. But then I had to rush off as I was feeling sick. I went back to the dormitory, where I saw I was looking a bit dishevelled. Mr Kazocins espied me and gave me two Alka-Seltzers. I decided to freshen up and change again. I put on my blue trousers and red jumper. When I returned to the bonfire, Valdis had given up and gone to bed. But I managed to stay up until 5 a.m., with some nice thoughts of him saying he loved me. He had called me 'darling' and told me he had liked me all week. We had ended with a kiss.

On Saturday 26 August I was up early, at 7.30 a.m., as the camp was ending at 9 a.m. Those going to Hereford had a bus pick them up. Dace and I were in no hurry to leave and wandered around until lunchtime. Around 2 p.m. my father arrived. Family friends, Mr and Mrs Fridenbergs, lived in the grounds, so we called in to see them with their chickens. On the way home we stopped in Hereford so that I could buy some souvenirs. I was so tired, and I had a nice hot bath when I got in.

The rest of the school holidays was spent doing homework and revision until school resumed on 4 September. A week later the school decided to take our measurements. At five feet three and three-quarters inches in height, I weighed eight stone two and a quarter pounds.

On 16 September the RAF held an air show at St Athan. My parents managed to book a flight for us on the pleasure trip, which was my first ever time up in a plane. We were up in the air for only ten minutes, which cost us fifteen shillings each. It was lovely. I couldn't feel the take-off at all and it was a joy to be up in the air. The landing was slightly bumpy. The plane held twenty-eight passengers. We left the show at 7 p.m., and because of the heavy traffic we didn't get home until 8.15 p.m. There was nothing worth watching on television, so I decided to go to bed early, and my parents went out again to visit Mr and Mrs Kalnins – good friends of theirs.

In school, on 25 September, I showed my sketchbook to Mrs Lawrence, our art teacher. She marked it as 'excellent work C', which was a commendation, and told me I should go to art college.

My father got us tickets for the Components Supper Dance held on 29 September. I decided I would wear my chiffon dress. Tickets had cost £1 each. We arrived an hour late at the Connaught Rooms of the Continental and had our own table with young men from my father's garage. There was Pat with his girlfriend (Susie), little Mike, Ken and a strange, weedy lad also called Mike who wore glasses and had brought a friend with him. There was a live band playing. I drank two Babychams and a snowball. I was very pleased when little Mike eagerly danced 'The Last Waltz' with me. Pat had left before us as by 1.30 a.m. he had drunk too much. We had an enjoyable evening and stayed until 2.15 a.m.

Although my parents could be nice to live with, we all fell out over the weekend. I wondered why my mother had ever agreed to marry my father as he was being totally unreasonable. However, I felt no sympathy for Mother, who seemed to be always complaining about her heart, as I thought it was all due to her fragile nerves.

The Latvian Song Festival was held in Shipley, near Bradford, on 7 October 1967. The ball started at 7.30 p.m. Mother and I changed into our dresses after arriving there. I wore my mini silver dress and shoes. Many were there from the Latvian summer camp, including Dace, Maya, Ilze and Ruta. At 12.30 a.m. we went on to a party held at the Lejins' family home. Someone tried to pair me up with a tall blonde young man, but we were both too embarrassed by that attempt. Everyone had too much to drink. The following morning, after breakfast, we went to the Latvian Club, where I saw more people that I knew. We then went back to the Lejins' home before leaving there at 5.30 p.m. My parents had fallen out again. Mother refused to navigate, resulting in my father losing his way back to Cardiff a few times.

At the end of the month we attended yet another dance. Our

friend and neighbour from number 11 was a policeman and we were invited to the police ball at the Ocean Club. Gordon Stowe was there with his wife's brother John, who was twenty-three years old although he looked and behaved much younger. At 10 p.m. Gordon went back home to collect his wife, Sylvia, who hadn't felt well earlier. I danced with John, who thought my black shiny dress was 'kinky'! He was very shy otherwise and had little to say. The dance finished at 1 a.m. John said how much he had enjoyed himself. We also saw Pat and Susie at the dance.

On Friday 3 November, our setter, Sunits, had her second birthday. Also in November, the Rowe family were very unhappy. Mike was going to marry a young lady called Lesley, and his parents thought he was throwing away his career and his future. They believed that Lesley's parents had manipulated Mike as he seemed to do whatever they told him to. However, the wedding still took place. My parents were invited. Afterwards they returned with Mr Rowe, who was very upset, and they were all grumpy.

During November Uncle Rolands asked me to help him out at his office. I typed some letters for him and also sorted out some labelling.

In December it was the turn of Spencer Bartlett to take my fancy! He was the son of neighbours who lived in a bungalow at 19 Lonsdale Road, which was behind the Rowes' house. I thought he was 'gorgeous', although five months younger than me. As he was so young, he could be annoying at times, and wasn't always polite. My mother thought he should only be a friend. I had a real crush on him, but decided not to encourage him. Spence would drop in to play records, then kiss me goodnight. His parents were very pleasant and were always happy to have me visit. When I wanted to see *Bonnie and Clyde* at the cinema, my parents invited Spence. Mother had a lot to do, so I went to see the film with Father and Spence, even though it was X-rated. Spence treated me to a bar of chocolate. It was a good, exciting film with a bloody ending and we enjoyed it. But Father wasn't too impressed, especially as there were some sexy romantic scenes. It was pouring with rain when we came out. We dropped Spence off at 8.30 p.m. – we were invited in, but we had to refuse as we had promised Granny we would visit her.

January 1968 was filled with revision and exams at school. The mock GCE O levels started on the 22nd. The following is a list of all my passes with their grades (1 was the highest grade and 5 the lowest pass before failure): English language, 3; maths (geometry), 2; biology, 3; French, 2; art (practical), 2.5; maths (arithmetic), 2; German, 2; physics, 2.5; English literature, 1.75; maths (algebra), 3; art (model drawing), 2.5; and art (theory and history), 2.5. In human biology we learned all about reproduction in man. Perhaps a little late for some of the pupils! The teacher didn't blush once while explaining it all to us. We were shown two films – *Man and Woman*, parts one and two – which described and showed the deed in full detail.

February was reasonably quiet. I did some more work for my uncle, who paid me nine shillings. Astey's used to be a popular rendezvous for friends. After meeting my friend Jan outside Boot's at 6 p.m., we had a pasty and orange squash for one shilling and sixpence, then went on to Mary's 'party'. She lived in a vicarage and we helped her clean the cellar. When I got home at 11 p.m., my hair was filthy with cellar dust.

In March Father went to see a clairvoyant with Mr Rowe and Mr Bartlett. The psychic accurately described my appearance in detail and told my father that I would wear a white coat and have something to do with the medical profession. Surprisingly, a week later I had an interview with the youth employment officer and decided I'd like to be a radiographer.

Another police ball was coming up and I needed a partner. I had seen Ian in Dad's garage when I had dropped in for a possible lift home. So I asked my father if he could find out whether Ian would like to come with us. It seemed he was willing and would call at our house in his red Mini. The dance was two days before my sixteenth birthday. After I washed my hair I tried to style ringlets, but that failed, so I put my hair up instead and wore my crochet two-piece. Ian Jones worked as a clerk for Midland Bank and he looked very different without grease on his face from helping Father at the garage. He arrived at 8 p.m. Then Gordon and Sylvia came to the house at 8.30 p.m. We all set off together, the ground covered in snow, to the Ocean Club. Ian's dark hair curled slightly at the nape, and he had huge brown eyes. Dishy! He would slightly touch my waist when we finished a dance, then he would put his arm around my waist. During the last waltz, he slowly drew me up to him until he had his chin against my cheek. When the dance was over, he held me closely. Then we all headed back to our cars. Ian didn't hide putting his arm around my waist, but Mother wasn't too happy and did her best to try and hang on to me. I decided to go home in Ian's car, and we arrived twenty minutes before my father, who had driven the long way round. I remained in the Mini with Ian when my parents went indoors. When we didn't go straight in, my father stormed out and yanked the car door open as he was not happy at my being alone with Ian. We were told to go into the house. Ian asked if I would like to go to the university dance with him. He said he would ring me to arrange the date. Ian liked 1940s jazz music and Glen Miller, as well as a strange mix of Rolling Stones, rock 'n' roll and Anita Harris. His hobbies included sailing, rallying and motor racing. He also went out every night. Finally, he left at 4 a.m., by which time my father had nodded off in the chair. Mother busily chatted with me and I didn't get to bed until 5.30 a.m. I couldn't get over Ian as I thought he was so lovely. But he was also eight years older than me.

I didn't see him again until 24 April, and I had spent every spare moment thinking about him. When I saw him my heart jumped and he said I looked beautiful. A week later he called to see me again. We had another date on 4 July. The following evening we went out for some drinks at The Buccaneer pub. When he saw me home he stayed until 1 a.m., then gave me a kiss. I really did like him. The next day he telephoned me and I missed not seeing him face-to-face. On 10 July he brought his best friend, Dick, to visit us, and the following day they both collected me from my school trip. For some reason, doubts began to creep in about our relationship, and I hoped that he wasn't making a fool of me.

On Friday 12 July the Howardian School Dance took place, and Ian agreed to partner me. I was left feeling disappointed due to his lack of manners. Both Ian and Dick came to visit the following Monday and Tuesday. Then on the 19th Ian rang to see if I'd like to go for a night drive. He lent me his record player on 22 July. On 5 August, after the city-centre shops closed, I had a wander and bumped into Ian. We walked together as far as Charles Street and he asked if he could take me out the following Friday. On that date we visited some friends of his – Diana and her husband, who lived in the Valleys. We then ended the evening having drinks at The Buccaneer and The Unicorn. I had been ordered home by 10.25 p.m., so Ian came in with me and stayed until 1 a.m.

There was no sign of Ian through September, even though it was his twenty-fourth birthday on the 13th. Sadly, I received no invitation to join him.

On 12 October Ian called in the morning just to collect his record player. I still liked him, but our dates were dwindling.

On Friday 22 November Ian came to visit me and my parents in the evening. Even though he stayed until 4 a.m., we didn't have any more dates.

Ian was probably my first real romance – my childhood sweetheart at only sixteen years of age. I was in love with Ian – really in love – but there was no depth to our relationship. We remained just good friends. I still liked him, but he no longer made my knees go weak or my heart tremble. He managed to kill the passion by keeping me at arm's length in the end. In later years, after he had married twice, he admitted that he stopped dating me out of respect for my father. Ian saw him as a father substitute, and was very fond of him. He had no wish to destroy that closeness by continuing to see me. Perhaps if he had known my true feelings for him, he might have acted differently, and he regretted that.

Anyway, it was a long time before I saw Ian again. He turned up at the house on New Year's Day in 1971, when he looked extremely dashing and my heart took a leap. However, he came with a young man called Duncan, who was a customer of my father's at the garage. By the time they went home at 5 a.m. I was absolutely smitten by Duncan, who was everything I had ever looked for in a man.

The 14th of April 1968 was Easter. We visited Granny and gave her potted flowers and a card I had made for her. As usual, I had to hunt for my Easter egg, which was hidden inside the record player. There was an extra gift of a blue handbag hidden behind my school briefcase. My friend Jeanette came to visit, as did Gordon and Sylvia, then Ken from my father's garage. During the holiday I babysat for Pam and John next door, who paid me seven shillings and sixpence to be there from 9.30 p.m. until 12.30 a.m. Their little girl was called Juliette and was easy to babysit. If she woke up, all I had to do was put a dummy in her mouth.

At school, in May, I tried discus throwing for the first time. I was so surprised by one of my throws, I said, "Beautiful!" quite loudly, not realising a teacher was standing behind me. She commented that I was a 'natural'.

We had a career school visit to the Royal Infirmary, which was really interesting. We were shown all the departments – nursing, radiography and physiotherapy. For me, radiography was the most interesting.

On Friday 10 May I called on Christine at 6.10 p.m. We went to see *Here We Go Round The Mulberry Bush*, which was X-rated. We enjoyed it, but also thought it was 'very kinky'! It finished at 10.20 p.m.

Two of my father's customers were French students and he invited them to visit us. Claire was a tall girl, twenty-one years old, five feet ten inches and very friendly. Her friend Josie was quieter and very pleasant. They tested me on my spoken French as my oral exam was on 28 May. I'd had some time off school as I was catching a lot of colds, and it wasn't easy to catch up with my studies.

I regularly bought the magazine *Fabulous* and had entered one of their competitions. They wanted a story written that included all the song titles on the Move's latest LP. Not only did they print my entry, but I also won a copy of the LP and a signed photo from the group. I was thrilled to bits.

I often took our red setter for walks, but she wasn't easy to handle as she was so boisterous. A council estate had just been built behind our house, on the other side of the stream and small wood, and people had started moving in. We walked to Roath Park Lake, and that is where Sunits fell in as she didn't realise that the water wasn't solid!

The 3rd of June was bank holiday Monday and my father decided we could all go to Porthcawl, taking Christine as well. Chris and I spent a fortune on the fairground rides; then we were picked up by two young men, who walked with us along the beach. Christine really liked her fella and arranged to meet him again.

On 10 June GCE O levels started. I seemed to manage having a social life as well as swotting and sitting my exams. On 11 June my school friend Mary Lloyd gave me a hamster as hers had had babies. I was ready with a cage I'd bought a couple of days earlier.

Mike Rowe came to visit us with his baby. His wife refused to see his parents because they didn't approve of the situation, which they described as 'complicated'. I never did find out why.

Saturday 22 June 1968 proved to be an important date in my life. My mother's cousin Juris came to visit with three American friends. One of them was a friendly young man called Sandy. Although not handsome, he was tall and fair, with a great personality, and he was the right age at eighteen years. It was a shame that they only stayed in the UK for a few days.

Midsummer's Night was celebrated in Almeley on Saturday 29 June. As usual, I took a fancy to a lad, and this time it was Barry after I patted his friend's dog! We didn't retire until 4.30 a.m., so I felt pretty tired all Sunday. The same week I had lost weight and was only seven stone eleven pounds. I also had my long hair cut to below shoulder-length, which upset my father.

On Monday 8 July exams were over and there was nothing to do in school except for sports day. Then on 11 July we went on a school trip to Exmoor. In Minehead a nice young man tried to chat me up, which was nice. It was a lovely outing, which lasted from 9 a.m. to 9 p.m.

I was very happy to receive an unexpected letter from Sandy on 13 July.

My last day in school was Thursday 18 July. Harlech Television came to film our school, and they had a dishy cameraman called Brian.

My father knew everyone as he was a very popular mechanic, and he succeeded in getting me a Saturday job. So on 20 July I had a go at working on the sweet counter of Newscards' shop in Llanrumney. It didn't go too well as I messed up the till. Ever since then tills have always worried me. It was a coincidence that Pam's mother also worked there. The highlight of the day was that some nice boys tried to chat me up. The following Saturday I attempted to work there again. I turned up late, which didn't help, and I was put to work in the card department. Believe it or not, I didn't bother to go again the following Saturday as it was too difficult to get there on public transport and, to my mind, probably the job wasn't worth the effort.

In July, I was still friendly with Josie and we went to see Walt Disney's *Jungle Book*. It was such a good film that we sat through it twice! Father gave Josie a lift home afterwards. That month I also saw *Camelot*. Franco Nero was gorgeous, the story weepy, and the songs and acting were beautiful. I liked the music so much that I bought the LP a couple of days later. Another film that was quite good was *The Happiest Millionaire*. It starred my childhood heart-throb Tommy Steele, and I remained a lifelong fan of his.

At the beginning of August my parents' friends Mr Taylor and his friend/companion Jekab visited us from Swansea. We drove them back home as that meant we could also visit Dzintra and her parents, Rose and Imants.

O-level results were published on 24 August. I managed to pass in seven subjects, which were English language, French,

German, maths, biology, English literature and art. After staring at an empty paper, my mind went blank; so it was no surprise that I failed in physics.

On Wednesday 28 August, my parents saw me off at the station as I was catching the 11.55-a.m. train from Cardiff to Plymouth. I shared the compartment with two older ladies, and my mother asked them to keep an eye on me! I reached my destination at 4.35 p.m., and was met at the station by my school friend Paula Finch. Her little sister, Sheila, was a bit of a raver (the very opposite of Paula) and every day there would be a few boys sitting on their garden wall waiting for her to emerge. We took it easy the next day then went shopping on Friday. We were chased around the Co-op by four males. At the cinema we saw *They Came from Outer Space*, which was shown with another film, which starred Rod Taylor and Dahlia Lavi. We were chatted up again! On Saturday Paula's parents took us sightseeing and we visited Looe, Polruan (an ancient fishing village) and Fowey – all very picturesque. There were many Frenchmen visiting the area. On Monday we drove around Dartmoor and visited Widecombe. The last few days were spent in Plymouth, seeing the museum and going to the top of the civic centre, from where I took some photos. On Thursday I crammed everything into my suitcase and headed for home.

I plucked up courage on 6 September to go and see my headmistress, Miss Curtis, who was supposed to be in school preparing for the start of term. However, she wasn't there, so I had to leave her a letter. I was supposed to be back at school doing A-level studies on 9 September. As I couldn't stand the thought of returning to school, which was too strict for my liking, I wrote that I had decided to leave and would no longer be studying French, biology and art.

On 11 September I attended art college to sit the entrance exam, which was not easy. I recall having to paint a still life, but it was stressed that our pictures were not to be as we saw the subject. They had to be abstract, which really wasn't my style. And the whole idea was that I would be accepted as a student so that I could study fashion design. Only two days later they let me know I had failed. I wasn't surprised as I hadn't done my best, but I didn't think I wasn't good enough to pass. I was very disappointed.

I had an interview on 3 October at 10.30 a.m. for the post of junior technician (draughtsman). To prepare I had to buy inks, paper and pens as I had to do drawings. The interview only lasted forty-five minutes. I had another interview the next day at 12.15 p.m. for the post of junior technician in the Royal Infirmary. I was confronted by a panel of four interviewers. It only lasted ten minutes and I felt I had no chance of a job offer there. Sure enough, four days later that was confirmed. I wasn't offered that job either. I was only applying for 'professional' vacancies as I was considered overqualified for basic employment.

On a happy note, I was now regularly communicating with Sandy, and on 28 September he enclosed a photo with his letter. He was a little overweight, but army training would help trim him down. A week later I wrote back to him, and on 19 October I was pleased to receive another letter from him, which was very nice.

Scott Walker was my idol, and on Wednesday 16 October I went to the Capitol to see him perform. I had Seat A51 in Block C in the dress circle, which cost me seventeen shillings and sixpence. The show started at 6.30 p.m. He wore a red corduroy suit and looked 'smashing'. When I waved to him (and I was the only one who did from my position) he smiled at me. Then later on, when singing another song, Scott pointed straight at me! I was flabbergasted. It was a very enjoyable show. Also appearing were The Casuals, who looked very nice. Love Affair, Paper Dolls and the Gun were also performing. But Scott was the best and was especially sexy when singing 'Amsterdam'.

On 20 October I wrote again to Sandy. I did more babysitting for Pam and John and on 25 October I looked after Julie from 7 p.m. to 1 a.m. She woke a number of times. I also had a little girl called Babs in my care that evening. She decided she didn't want me to emigrate as she liked me. (My father was always planning to move abroad.) I was paid fifteen shillings.

Out of interest, I checked my measurements on 30 October. At the age of sixteen and a half years, I weighed eight stone, and my figure was 35"–24"–36". I was five feet four and a half inches tall. By 7 December my weight had dropped to seven stone eleven pounds, which was considered underweight by a few folk. At that time my clothes size was 12. If you were 32"–22"–34", then you were a size 10. There were no smaller sizes in the boutiques; so if you were tiny, a visit to a children's department had to be considered.

During October I had a number of letters from Sandy, who was based in Fort Campbell in Kentucky. Uncle Rolands saw some of the pictures I had drawn for Sandy and asked me to do some designs for him.

On Sunday 10 November I went with my father to visit our old neighbour in Kimberley Road, Mr Wicks. I also saw my old 'boyfriend' David, who had changed a lot since his short-trousers days! He was now quite an agreeable young man.

There was an announcer called Roger Scott on Harlech Television. I thought he was 'super' and decided to write him a fan letter. You can imagine how happy I was to receive a lovely reply from him.

Through November and December Sandy wrote a number of letters and also enclosed another photo in one of them. For Christmas I sent him a boxed card.

In 1968 I also achieved another feather in my cap by attending a course at the Pat David Model and Charm School. On 15 July I commenced my training in Parkwood House at 52 Charles Street in Cardiff. The agency was also based at 77 New Bond Street, London.

We studied applying make-up, which was quite interesting. We did keep-fit exercises and learned how to walk properly, and also how to speak well. Adverts were acted out and I did a spoof for the trousers I was wearing. We combined dance with walking at the same time on the catwalk and learned about social sciences. I was physically flexible, which was an advantage. I was able to demonstrate how to do turns. We did photographic posing, but I didn't find that particularly enjoyable. There were correct ways to wear a shawl, carry an umbrella and remove one's coat. Also I could display shoes the right way on the catwalk. I enjoyed our 'wig night', when I tried on a gorgeous shoulder-length wig (usual price eleven guineas). It suited my colouring and had a beautiful texture.

The finale day of modelling was on 27 August. Having attended classes twice a week, it was wonderful to be told I was the best in the class. My modelling technique was 'very good' after being marked on facial expression, entrances and exits, model walk, make-up, posture and photographic posing. Pat David's 'general remarks' were 'Lolita has extremely good co-ordination with hands and feet. A very pleasant girl with a nice personality.'

I applied for many jobs and attended a number of interviews, unsuccessfully, including one with the Pearl Assurance Company on 29 November.

There was another police ball on Monday 9 December and I went to the Rhymney Breweries with my parents, the Stowes, the Dymonds and, amazingly, my old friend David Wicks. We all had great fun. A group called the Lee Brothers entertained and I flirted with the drummer, who gave me his broken drumstick, which I kept as a souvenir for many years. The evening ended at 2 a.m.

The past year had its ups and downs and if I wasn't falling out with my mother and father, then they were falling out with each other. Mother said I was 'thoughtless' and Father often picked on me. It got me down as I always felt I had good intentions, but hid my true feelings. Having left school, I was happy that a lot of friends kept in touch. I either saw or heard from Averil Leimon, Valmai James, Angela Dumazel, Sandra Smith, Christine Aggett, Juliette Binmore and Vanessa Wilson. Christine Samuel and Paula Finch wrote regularly, and of course Christine Lloyd was my regular friend.

On 24 December my parents and I left home at 4 p.m. to travel all the way to Sheffield. There were snowstorms around

Birmingham. We were staying with Jekab and Mr Taylor, who lived there together, having moved north. Jekab gave me a gold-coloured scarf, and Mr Taylor gave me a cosmetics set. On Boxing Day we went to a party at the Bradford Latvian Club and I met two young men who both kissed me goodbye! Awo Subris gave me his address in Baildon, near Shipley, and we corresponded for a while.

On 1 January 1969 I received a letter from the Yorkshire Insurance Company, offering me an interview. I responded quickly, the following day. The interview was held on 6 January at 3 p.m. The offices were very pleasant, in Windsor Place. The manager was Scottish and we seemed to get on very well. If I was interested in accepting the job, I was to let him know. I really felt I had a ninety-nine-per-cent chance of being officially offered the post. As I felt so positive, I wrote to them the next day to say I would accept. I couldn't believe it when on the Friday I received a letter saying that, due to changed circumstances, they could no longer take me on. I was very disappointed as I had been looking forward to working there.

On 4 January the Vizbulis family arrived at our house at 6.45 p.m., and we all went to see *Sleeping Beauty on Ice* at 7.30 p.m. It was spectacular. Our good family friend an Indian young man called Sammi opened his new restaurant, The Seventh Veil. To support his business we enjoyed a tasty tandoori chicken meal there, then returned home. Our visitors left at 2.45 a.m.

On the Sunday I helped Father sort out his business papers and he paid me ten shillings for my efforts. We then visited Gordon at 9.30 p.m.

I seemed to be always buying new clothes, C&A being one of my favourite stores. One purchase was a cape-style raincoat which cost only twenty-nine shillings. In Wallis I treated myself to a fur coat costing £29 8s. in their sale. It was a zip-up real-cony fur coat, which felt very luxurious. I was also keen on knitting and bought eight ounces of blue crimp nylon at one shilling and nine pence per ounce to knit a jumper with. I used to help my uncle with some of his orders and was still in demand to babysit next door, where I started knitting my top. I helped my uncle to stick numbers he'd printed on to game-machine wheels. My knitting progressed well and I also managed to write some letters.

On Saturday 18 January 'Uncle' George (Cousin Juris) was getting married to a beautiful girl called Mildred Rosario Ojeda in St Croix, one of the US Virgin Islands. We were invited to the wedding being held at 5 p.m. It would have been a dream to go, but we didn't have the finances to travel somewhere so exotic in those days.

On Monday 20 January I had yet another interview. This time it was for the post of stockroom clerk in C&A. But I failed to be offered the job. Mother wasn't well for a few days, so I cooked dinner and made butterfly cakes and cornflake crackles. On the 26th my parents were rowing again. As usual, it was my father's fault as he didn't seem to care whom he upset. I argued with him as well, as he often thought the worst of me and was very quick-tempered. As a husband he was not good for Mother – his only good point was that he earned enough money to look after us. I felt sure that if Mother could earn money and support herself, she would have left him. I spent many days sticking numbers on wheels for my uncle – a very tedious job. Mother was also probing me about Sandy. All I could comment was that he had a nice personality, but I didn't know him well enough to decide how much I liked him.

On Friday 31 January I had two interviews. At 2.20 p.m. I sat in front of three men in Cardiff Royal Infirmary who wished to employ a student technician. Then at 7 p.m. I had a scary interview at Studio 91, where they were looking for a photographic model. It went quite well and I was there for about half an hour while they took four photos of me. I walked home. I was told Sunits had escaped again that day, and luckily she was found by a boy in Gabalfa.

I often went shopping in town with my parents on Saturdays. In BHS I bought myself a white fur hood at twenty-nine shillings and eleven pence, and a pink woollen thin knitted dress for only nineteen shillings and eleven pence. I saw my friend Janette Thomas, who worked in Boot's. On the way home we would pop in and see Granny. On 2 February we left home at 6.15 p.m., even though it was snowing, to visit the Vizbulis family. We stayed there until 12.30 a.m., and were home again by 2.15 a.m. It was very cold. Again I failed to be offered a job – this time the one at the hospital. I was still waiting to hear about the modelling job. Mother and Father surprised me by encouraging me to marry Sandy! But I had no intention of marrying anyone yet.

On Thursday 6 February I set off for my favourite disco, Top Rank, where I met Angela at 7.45 p.m. We had lots of dances with young men, and we also attracted a few admirers. I accepted a date for Saturday with a blonde bloke called Mike. My father picked us up and took Angela home first, after midnight. The weather was snowy and it was freezing cold. Mother was still nagging me about Sandy, saying if I didn't marry him, then I wouldn't be marrying anyone else either. I wasn't against marriage, but at sixteen years of age I wanted to date lots of nice boys before I settled down. The following Thursday I met Angela at 8.15 p.m., again at Top Rank. We saw a lot of girls we knew. An Indian lad kept pestering me and he commented on how beautiful and how pretty I was, and said he loved my company. I tried to lose him, but failed, so I ended up telling him I had a boyfriend. He told me to forget him. Angela couldn't shake off her bloke either. I managed to lose Syed in the crowd, then Angela's dance partner, called Fred, found someone else for me to dance with. When we left, Angela went home with Fred, and my father collected me.

The whole of the UK was in chaos on 19 February as there were snowdrifts, avalanches, gales and floods. It just snowed and snowed all day. Plans for dancing had to be abandoned. I managed to take Sunits out for a couple of walks. I did more knitting and also made a pattern for a wrap-over dress I was going to attempt to sew.

On 24 February I had an interview with Miss Owens, my officer at the Youth Employment Bureau. She was very pleasant and helpful, and arranged for me to attend an interview at the zoology department in the University College at 5 p.m. the next day. All seemed to go well and I hoped I'd left a good impression – I felt I'd said all the right things. I was shown around the laboratories, which had a variety of animals in cages. The rabbits, ducks, gulls, chickens, rats, mice, locusts, snails, toads, etc., were all used for experiments. I then popped in to see Granny at 6 p.m. I only stayed forty-five minutes and she gave me thirteen shillings as a bit of pocket money. She loved to give me Smarties as the advert on television said to buy some for Lulu, and Lulu was also my nickname.

On Wednesday I sewed my red dress together, and I wore it to Top Rank the following evening. We had an enjoyable time and met a couple of nice boys.

My fortunes changed on Saturday 1 March as I had an interview in the Royal Infirmary at 9.50 a.m. I didn't realise it was with the same people who'd seen me before. However, this time it all seemed to go better and the post was to work in their medical unit. Gordon saw me walking towards home on Newport Road and gave me a lift home at 10.30 a.m. Mother was not well again, so I helped Father cook dinner. We were having boiled potatoes with roast beef. On 3 March I had a telephone call from St David's Hospital. The secretary told me I had not been offered the job I had gone for. However, perhaps I would be interested in working in their Asthma and Allergy Research Unit? If yes, then my interview would be at 2.15 p.m. the next day. I decided to attend, and met a Miss Thomas at St David's Hospital. I felt a bit dithery, but she was very pleasant. I didn't realise that Christine Gibbon from school also worked there. If I was interested, the job was mine! I had to let them know my decision. I went to the Youth Employment Bureau to discuss my insurance card and then called at the garage to ask Father for a lift home. I babysat again for next door and earned ten shillings for being there for four and a half hours. I must have been very useful to them as I was asked to babysit again the next day.

On Thursday 6 March I received an official letter offering me the job of student medical laboratory technician in the

Asthma and Allergy Research Unit of St David's Hospital. The laboratory was actually based in Cardiff Royal Infirmary. Angela and I went to Top Rank again, but as she had to catch a bus home we only stayed until 10.45 p.m. The next day I collected my insurance card from the Youth Employment Bureau. Miss Thomas also rang me to make arrangements for my first day at work.

On Monday 10 March, at long last, my working life began. I rose at 8 a.m. and met Christine Gibbon by the porter's lodge of the Royal Infirmary at 9 a.m. in my white coat. I had a good morning and had to deal with adding dichloromethane to samples of urine. In the afternoon I had my medical at St David's, where they took an X-ray, and my thumb was pricked by a very nice young man. By 3.45 p.m. I was back at the infirmary and did more to help Christine. Although she had only worked there for five or six months, she was training me. I was home by 5.30 p.m. and was absolutely starving!

On Tuesday I managed to find my own way to the laboratory. In the afternoon Dr Shaboury took Christine and me to St David's with samples. We had to catch the bus back and then had a very busy day. Wednesday was quite a good day at work, but it took me a while to get the hang of it. On Thursdays Christine went to technical college, so I had June keep watch over me. We worked with plasmas, and we did forty-six that day. I had to work hard as I was left to do quite a bit on my own. But I quite enjoyed it so far. Friday was not easy. In the morning Dr Shaboury asked me questions and I had to describe the plasma method. I only just scraped through. He then went on to describe the principle of the urine-and-plasma experiments, which was rather complicated, to say the least. For me it was a relief to stop for lunch!

Dzintra Vizbulis and Rita Likums had been having confirmation classes in Swansea, and it was decided that I would join them for the lessons. So on Saturday 15 March my father took me to Dzintra's home. Mother wasn't feeling well, so she stayed at home. At 5 p.m. we went to church, then on to Rita's house, where our dean, Mr Mužiks, gave a confirmation talk for a couple of hours. Rita wanted me to stay overnight, but Father wanted to get back home. I was never christened, and it seemed I had to be before I could be confirmed, so that had to be planned too.

On Monday I was back in work, but things didn't go well. I was all thumbs, and I managed to break one test tube, knocked over a bell jar and dropped a glass stopper on the floor. A very cold and rainy day. I managed to oversleep on Wednesday and was ten minutes late for work. Dr Shaboury made me nervous as he was closely watching me pipetting and I ended up having a tension headache. On Thursday I was on my own in work and spent all morning doing readings on the spectrometer. Then in the afternoon I had to do some cleaning and also used dichlo, then made sodium hydroxide solution. I had to work on Saturday mornings and would go into town to do some shopping with Christine sometimes.

On Saturday 22 March I went with Angela to Top Rank, where we had lots of dances and quite a few were with sailors. Around 10 p.m. I met a very nice young man called Rolf. He considered me a rarity as I had not just beauty and brains, but personality too. I have to admit I felt very flattered.

I liked Rolf enough to go on a few dates with him. We went to the cinema and one of the films we saw was *Sweet Charity* in the Capitol. It wasn't a bad film, especially when snuggled up to Rolf in the back row. Another film we saw was *Cat Balou*, showing in the Globe Cinema, and that was very good and funny. We liked to dance at Top Rank as well. In between seeing each other, Rolf would ring me or send a letter. It was a shame, but we drifted apart quite soon.

I settled quite well into my job and Dr Shaboury didn't bother me too much, especially as Christine seemed to trust me to work correctly. I also had my first pay for my first three weeks of work as a technician. I received £23 3s. 11d. in my pay packet, which put a smile on my face.

My babysitting services were still being required for Pam and John next door, on a regular basis. Six hours of my services would earn me sixteen shillings, but often I wasn't there for very long. Their baby was well behaved, and generally it was easy money as I could have coffee and a sandwich, and watch television or play their vinyl albums. I recall a favourite singer of theirs was Barbra Streisand.

My confirmation was arranged for Saturday 30 August 1969, and the lessons would continue until then. It would be a big celebration, and we girls needed to buy lovely white gowns for the event.

My Sandy was no longer a passing phase. He was to play a major part in the next chapter of my life. Our letters became more intense as a result of getting to know each other. His real name was John B. Curtis junior, and his home was Monon Valley Farm – a large cattle ranch in Monon, Indiana. Born on 3 March 1950, he had enlisted in the army and was due to leave in October for his new home, Fort Campbell in Kentucky. I had become his 'sweetheart', and I felt privileged to be able to write to this special young man in my life and received letters sealed with kisses. . . .

> "I have gotten my orders telling me that I am reporting to Vietnam. I've decided that I really don't care too much about anything they can do to me.
> If I get killed there, what would you like me to leave you?"